The Fall of Richmond

THE FALL

LOUISIANA STATE

REMBERT W. PATRICK

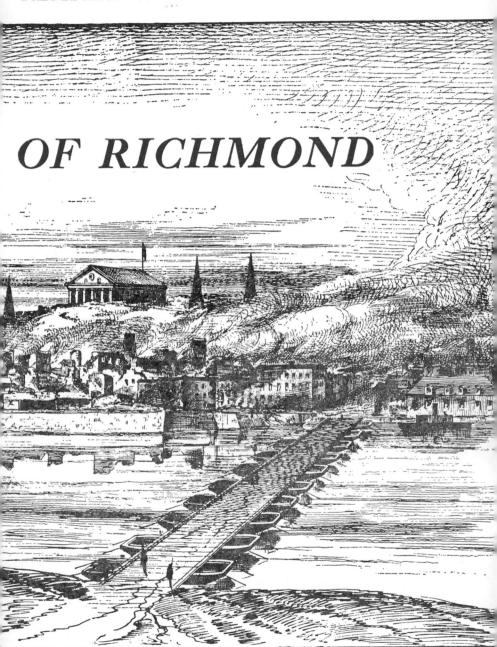

OF RICHMOND

UNIVERSITY PRESS • BATON ROUGE

TO MY FIRST WIFE

PREFACE

A summary of the contents of this volume was given in 1959 at Louisiana State University as the twenty-first series of the Walter Lynwood Fleming lectures. After the first lecture President Troy H. Middleton asked: " Why did the leaders of the Confederacy not foresee the fall of Richmond and have plans for continued resistance from some other city? "

The answer to this question, and to most historical queries, is complex. In 1862 and in 1865 Jefferson Davis and his advisers anticipated the need to move from Richmond to some other Southern city. Months before April, 1865, the employees of bureaus were transferred to Columbia, alternate supply routes were mapped, prisoners of war were exchanged or moved south, archives were boxed, and officials were ready for hasty departure. All of these acts, however, were meaningless. General William T. Sherman had cut the heart of the Old South and General Ulysses S. Grant had brought General Robert E. Lee to the point of surrender. Other than temporary asylum the Confederate leaders had no haven east of the Mississippi River. Without armies, matériel, and transportation the Confederacy was doomed. Optimistic prophesies of Jefferson Davis reassured few Southerners.

In reality leaders and people organize and work for victory rather than defeat. Before 1865 no white people of the United States had known defeat in war. Even today

v

arming for victory stimulates enthusiasm and patriotism, planning for civil defense meets with indifference or resistance. Hints that officials are considering action in case of defeat brings vigorous condemnation from us characteristically optimistic Americans.

So it was almost one hundred years ago with the people of Richmond. They worked for, hoped for, and lived for victory; and defeat came with unexpected suddenness to a people unprepared physically or mentally for failure. The story of the evacuation, capture, and occupation of Richmond is unique in American history.

Sources for this narrative of a doomed city were gathered with the aid of librarians of the University of Florida, University of North Carolina, Virginia State, and New York Public libraries; the National Archives; the Library of Congress; and the Confederate and Valentine museums. I am grateful to Edwin A. Davis and the other members of the History Department at Louisiana State University for the privilege of delivering the Fleming Lectures. Marilyn Cox and Nancy Gray copied and recopied the manuscript, and my wife, Eleanor, gave constructive criticism in addition to care in reading proof.

REMBERT W. PATRICK

Gainesville, Florida
March, 1960

CONTENTS

ILLUSTRATIONS

The Fall of Richmond

(*I*)

EVACUATION, *April 2, 1865*

MORNING

IT WAS ALMOST dawn before Richmond slept. Even then it was a troubled sleep, no more than a pause between the end of one day and the beginning of another. The roll of cannon and the staccato of muskets from the direction of Petersburg ceased. Moist air muffled the few hurried footsteps as darkness shrouded gaunt buildings in lonely streets. Stars twinkled out their last moments of brilliance above the capital of the Confederacy.

In the morning quiet, every sound had meaning. The bass rumblings of wagons drawn by tired mules indicated heavy loads were being hauled to the Danville Railroad station. Drivers' curses profaned the cathedral hush of the city. The rattle and clank of briskly moving vehicles told of empty wagons leaving the station for warehouses and governmental offices.

Gaslights flickered in the War Department building where telegraphers were translating the clicking of keys into meaning. Recent reports had been foretelling the fate of Richmond. General Robert E. Lee's dispatches had emphasized his thin and wavering lines at Petersburg. Rain and mud had for a time prevented a major thrust against him by General U. S. Grant, but then the incessant rains had ended. Sun and wind had dried the land on Saturday, April 1, and now Lee was powerless to stay the advancing Grant. His telegraph messages had called for help, but no more help existed. The available manpower of the Confederacy had disappeared in wounds and death, in hopelessness and desertions.

Faithful soldiers guarded the defenses of Richmond. They walked their silent rounds, alert, still ignorant of impending defeat at Petersburg. Relatively few comrades slept under their care, for the battlefront and other services claimed every possible man. Warehouses, the arsenal, the powder magazine, prisons, industries, and public safety—all these required guards. On a miniature fleet of seven ships on the James River near Rockett's Landing a few sailors held the remnant of a never-powerful Confederate navy. Teamsters, ordnance and iron workers, commissary agents, railroad men, and officers and cadre at the capital further reduced the defensive forces of Richmond.

For more than a year, in time of crisis, companies composed of older men and boys taken from governmental offices had manned the breastworks surrounding Richmond. Never had the need for them been so great as on this morning of April 2. Thus, in the predawn, appointed sentinels moved through the quieted city to grasp and pull bell ropes which would call reluctant men to duty.

At 6:00 A.M. the ringing bells awakened slumbering Richmond. Clerks, turned soldiers for the day, splashed sleep away at washbowls and pulled on worn trousers. They buttoned patched shirts, slipped on frayed coats, and rummaged for protection against possible rain. Cool, moist air greeted them. Apprehensively they searched the reddening sky for signs of the weather. It was too early to predict the day. A bright sun could clear the misty air, or steady rain might fall from gray skies. All the while the clerk-soldiers grumbled their discontent. Often they had been called out for defense, and seldom had they been needed. Now on Sunday, their one day of rest, they must serve in what they felt would undoubtedly be rain and mud.

Slowly the men went out into the streets and moved to their appointed musters. There was more activity in Richmond now. Sounds of marching men and creaking wagons resounded in the streets. Bright sunrays, clearing the thin fog, promised clear skies. In the drier atmosphere noise seemed to travel faster and further and to reverberate against walls and buildings.

In his bedroom in the Confederate White House at Twelfth and Clay streets Jefferson Davis was alone. His wife's absence symbolized the precarious situation of Richmond. Days before, she and the children had left the capital and, under the care of Burton H. Harrison, the President's private secretary, they were now traveling somewhere to the south. Back in the late spring of 1862 Davis had similarly sped his family from the apparently doomed city. But then Lee and "Stonewall" Jackson had saved Richmond. Could Lee alone do it again? Jackson, J. E. B. Stuart, and other capable military leaders were now casualties of war. Moreover, only a shell now remained of the once-powerful defensive Army of Northern Virginia. Thinned by casualties and having few replacements, that army could not begin to match the human resources of Grant's forces. It suffered from scarcities of food and clothing, transportation facilities were inadequate to move available matériel to points of its need, and the men's morale was nearing the breaking point. Already Lee knew that his defensive victories of the past belonged to history. They could not be repeated. He reported as much to Jefferson Davis.

Davis, too, realized on that morning of April 2 that Richmond must be evacuated. He had already prepared for the inevitable; as early as May, 1864, preparations had been made to move the government to some other city should Richmond become untenable. A few bureaus had been transferred to more southerly cities. Beginning in March, 1865, governmental archives had been packed in boxes and shipped away from the capital. The families of some governmental officials had gradually left for destinations further south. Yet much remained to be done. Complete evacuation could never be accomplished until the hour of final necessity.

Plans had been made to meet that hour. Cabinet members and heads of bureaus had given the requisite orders. Essential records would be packed for shipment, and the others would be destroyed. The remaining gold of the Confederate treasury was to be sent under guard to the Danville Railroad station where trains would be in waiting for it, as well as for the archives and for officials of the government.

There was little more that Davis could do to speed evacuation. Then, there was always the hope that Lee's dispatches would bring reprieve. The President of the dying and unrecognized Confederacy washed, and combed his hair. He asked his Negro butler for a good dark suit and planned to attend the eleven o'clock services at St. Paul's Episcopal

Church. To Richmond Davis would appear calm, as though the loss of the capital was no more than a minor incident in the life of the Confederacy. Often in the course of four years he had suffered from excruciating pain caused by a number of ills, but this morning his health was good. Though almost blind in one eye, he felt young in body and ready to meet new trials. He ate breakfast and then conferred with aides. Unfortunately the news from Lee at Petersburg gave no hope for Richmond. The President prepared for church.

Other governmental officials spent the morning in various ways. Secretary of the Treasury George A. Trenholm remained in bed, suffering from an acute stomach disorder. His illness of some duration had kept Mrs. Trenholm in Richmond, and of all the cabinet members only he had the comforting presence of his wife. John H. Reagan, the Postmaster General, ate a frugal breakfast and hurried to the War Department. The unpolished, self-made Texan was brisk and demanding. Neither he nor his wife, while she lived, had been accepted by the " cultured society " of Richmond. What could one expect from uncouth Texas frontiersmen? was the caustic comment of Virginia matrons. But Reagan's sincerity and devotion to the Confederacy had never been questioned by anyone. Judah P. Benjamin, stout, dark, and immaculate, also walked to the War Department. Perhaps the ablest of the cabinet members, he had served as Attorney General and as Secretary of War before his appointment to the State Department. More than any other official he knew that the " Confederacy was war," and he hurried to the source which would report life or death. Benjamin's wife had visited Richmond once during the war, and had set virtuous tongues wagging about her affair with a handsome captain. She had lived in Paris, except for brief visits to New Orleans, and to Paris she had returned, where no puritanism limited one's freedom. Richmond society leaders felt sorry for Benjamin and enjoyed his wit and stories, but most Southerners condemned him as the Jewish evil genius of the Confederacy.

At the War Department Reagan and Benjamin joined the Secretary of War, John C. Breckinridge. The young, handsome, former Vice-President of the United States was tall and had a pleasing face which was set off by a long drooping mustache. He possessed a keen sense of humor, a cordial manner, a chivalry which endeared him to women, and a tremendous capacity for the consumption of his favorite Kentucky bourbon. He combined energy and indolence, but on the morning of April 2 he walked nervously to and fro while awaiting dispatches from the front. George Davis, the Attorney General, probably remained at his house that morning. This kind, gentle, friendly man possessed a genius for winning friends, and as a gentlemen of the old school he would refrain from adding to the confusion at the War Department. On the contrary, gregarious Stephen R. Mallory, the Secretary of the Navy, would not hesitate to voice his opinions. Although severely criticized in the South for his failure to build a navy which could break the blockade of Southern ports, he was noted in Richmond for glib anecdotes and the enjoyment of good living. He ate a hearty breakfast and probably stopped at the Navy Department before attending Mass at the Roman Catholic church.

The early morning brought no unusual excitement into the lives of state and local officials. At the governor's mansion William " Extra Billy " Smith breakfasted with his wife and daughter. His success in buying food and selling it at fair prices for the benefit of Richmonders was a particular source of pride with him. A very talkative man, he probably explained to his family again how his work had checked inflation. Eighty-year-old Mayor Joseph Mayo felt the weight of responsibility, for if Lee's army failed, Mayo would have the duty of surrendering Richmond. Confederate and state officials planned to run rather than to stay and be captured. Many members of the Virginia legislature questioned the advisability of remaining in the city and wondered what meetings or laws could accomplish in such a crisis. Former Governor John Letcher would remain in the capital to give advice whenever consulted. Although not a Virginian, John A. Campbell, the Assistant Secretary of War and a former Associate Justice of the United States Supreme Court, was considering means by which Virginia could act to terminate the war. And with this aim in mind he decided to stay in Richmond should the city be evacuated.

To the southeast of Richmond, at City Point, Virginia, President Lincoln smiled as he read telegram after telegram. For more than four years he had lived for the restoration of the Union. Now he shared the good news by relaying information to his Secretary of War, Edwin M. Stanton, in Washington. The President wrote that last night Philip Sheridan's Fifth Army Corps had captured three brigades of infantry, a train of wagons, several batteries, and thousands of prisoners; this morning Grant had ordered a general attack and the Confederate lines were broken. " All looks highly favorable," Lincoln concluded. He ended an additional and exceptionally good report with " all seems well with us, and everything quiet just now." As the hour approached in which all Americans, whether then realizing it or not, were to triumph in reunion, the great-hearted President thrilled to the prospect of success.

Few residents of Richmond knew of the impending evacuation. Of the famed wartime hostesses only the wealthy, dark-eyed, exotic beauty, Mrs. Robert C. Stanard, remained in the capital. Mrs. Thomas Jenkins Semmes, wife of the Louisiana senator who had expended more than $30,000 on food and entertainment in 1864, had already departed. Her popular charades would no longer compete with Mrs. Stan-ard's salon, the meeting place of cabinet members, generals, and the intelligentsia of Richmond. Single girls and young matrons that morning gave more attention to their depleted wardrobes, to the selection of dresses for church, than to rumors of evacuation. But the beautiful Hetty Cary Pegram, a former leader of the younger set, cared little about life. She and her sister Jennie had escaped from Baltimore in the early months of the war and with their cousin Constance had become known as the "Cary Invincibles." Constance Cary wrote poetry, was active in social affairs, and had become engaged to Burton Harrison, the secretary of President Davis. Hetty Cary had been the reigning beauty of Richmond. Her titian-haired loveliness and magnificently proportioned form moved a New Orleans reporter to write: "You have never seen—and probably [will] never see again so beautiful a woman." Late in January of 1865 she had been married to dashing officer John Pegram, had spent a three-week honey-moon with him in makeshift housing near the battlefront, and had wept in February at his funeral. Grief and expecta-tion were neighbors in Richmond. Young, attractive Betty Saunders expected her Colonel Walter Herron Taylor to rush to the city to marry her that afternoon, as he had promised. After the ceremony she hoped to find temporary quarters near the front to be with her husband, who was on General Lee's staff.

Older women anticipated or dreaded coming events. Elizabeth Van Lew in her lonesome mansion prayed for peace and the restoration of the Union which she loved and for which she worked during the war. This small, erect woman in her early forties, with her intense facial expression and bright blue eyes framed by ringlets of brown hair, had often visited Federal prisoners of war at Libby Prison and given them food and encouragement. Her imposing house, which she had inherited from her wealthy merchant father, had been a Union haven in Confederate Richmond. In the outskirts of the city Emma Mordecai presided over her brother's plantation house, dreading the future but never doubting her ability to protect her two feminine relatives or to manage her slaves. In her more than fifty years she had faced uncertainties with courage and her experience as a schoolteacher gave her confidence. Whatever thoughts her slaves held about freedom, these ideas did not hinder them in the performance of routine duties for their mistress.

Food and the enjoyment of the first warm day of spring filled the minds of slaves, free Negroes, and the mass of white people. Seldom did their breakfasts include more than grits and bacon grease. But the April sun dulled unpleasant memories of a cold winter with little wood, less coal, and threadbare bedding. So tired of war and so near starvation were many poor citizens that any change would be welcomed. Although they believed the propaganda of Yankee atrocities, they also envied the better-fed, better-clothed, and better-housed Northern enemy. If there were means to control Negroes other than slavery, most of the poorer white people would welcome the United States army.

The thoughts of the Richmond Negroes varied with individual circumstances. Slaves who were awaiting sale and possible transportation to more southerly points recalled the pleasant days in Richmond, and feared change. Thomas, a slave of Julie Handsford, lay on his stomach to ease the pain of a raw, bloodstained back. Only yesterday in the mayor's court he had been tried on a charge of stealing $1,000 worth of varnish from J. W. Salterwhite, and even though the evidence did not justify conviction, he was whipped as a warning against larceny. Barbara Clora of Caroline County also ministered to her wounds. She had claimed on Saturday that she was a free Negro, and the court had ordered her whipped for " being at large." Some slaves talked of freedom. Would the Northern army bring it, and what was freedom? Was it Saturday afternoon and Sunday come every day? Was it a time of rest, of play, of music and dancing with plenty of good things to eat and no responsibility? And because slavery never schooled anyone for freedom, few slaves could comprehend the responsibilities of a new status. Free Negroes worried about feeding their families with flour selling at $1,000 per barrel in Confederate money, corn at $100 per bushel, fat back at $18 per pound, and eggs at a dollar each. The members of two Negro companies which had drilled on Saturday afternoon under command of white officers and before curious spectators, including members of the Virginia legislature, recalled derogatory remarks of men who opposed arming slaves and rewarding them with freedom in return for their military service. The gray uniforms and the attention received did not erase the doubts of these adventurous colored troops.

Front-line combatants, still near Petersburg but already retreating that Sunday morning, mulled over vivid recollections of recent battles. First Sergeant Berry Greenwood Benson shuddered as he recalled the dark, threatening clouds on the night of March 30, and the march along roads already tramped into muddy slush by thousands of boots. As his company had left winter quarters that night, the soldiers were depressed by the burdens of war. The power of the enemy was by then so plain, Benson remembered, that the men hung their heads, stumbled along in despair, and agreed among themselves that they could fight but little longer. Why should fighting continue, they questioned, and men die for a hopeless cause? Yet the following day they remained on the picket line without rations. Suddenly a Federal soldier came charging. As he neared the Confederate line he was repeatedly ordered to halt and surrender, but unheeding he rushed onward and was shot. The Confederate soldiers gazed at the lifeless, bleeding body and speculated. Some said the Yankee was drunk, while others declared him crazy. The incident and resulting arguments relieved the boredom of war.

The following morning Benson had watched the enemy giving way before an advancing Confederate force. The Federals ran through the woods, stopping behind trees to fire and hurrying off again, until friend and foe disappeared in the deeper and more distant forest, and the sound of musketry grew fainter and fainter. But soon there came a fresh roar as the battle changed. Reinforcements checked advancing Confederates; sounds of battle increased again as the Federals reappeared. Again the two lines passed the rifle pits from which Benson watched, and the Confederates fled into breastwork defenses. Then in double line the Federals turned toward the rifle pits with their flags waving in the breeze. Although Confederate fire converged on them from an arc of more than 180 degrees, the blue-coated soldiers continued to advance. As the fire increased and the distance lessened, they fell into the covering grass, but courageous officers remained standing, flashing their swords and urging their men forward. The prone color-bearers held their flags aloft, and the Confederates concentrated their fire on the banners. Down went a flag as a bullet found the color-bearer, but up it rose. Down again, up again, down again, up again, the flags continued to tumble and rise, with the men hugging the ground and the officers waving their swords.

Benson fired his seven-shot Spencer rifle so rapidly he had to stop to let it cool. Near him his comrades fell one by one from the enemy fire. Now the Federals rose and streamed across the open field straight at the rifle pits. Their numbers overwhelmed the defenders. Benson and his comrades held until the final charge and then fled through a tangle of fallen trees and prickly bush back to the main breastworks.

That night, April 1, the thinly manned Confederate line had shifted from point to point to meet enemy thrusts. Benson listened to the Federals trampling among the bushes. Then he fired toward the sounds. He heard not only the snap of twigs and the swish of moving branches, but also voices speaking an alien language. Once some of the opponents came so close they were forced to surrender. They were German-Americans who spoke no English.

This morning then, the morning of April 2, probably about the time Jefferson Davis was getting up, the sharpshooters of Benson's command moved forward again, and while on picket duty they received orders to join a general retreat. At 3:30 A.M. the Federals had breached the main defenses of Petersburg. The corps commander, General A. P. Hill, had been killed. Petersburg had to be evacuated.

The sergeant and a few other men remained behind to break abandoned rifles, holding them by the stocks and swinging the barrels against trees to bend them and make them unusable. Then the men joined the heartbreaking movement. Benson met a few soldiers on the retreat, and they moved silently or sullenly down the breastworks, each one following the man before him. The retreat from Petersburg gained momentum.

Some of the sharpshooters brought up the rear to look for stragglers. They found one seated in a cabin before an open fire, cooking a hoecake in a dirty frying pan. Around him lay a pile of blankets, oilcloths, overcoats, knapsacks, and other plunder. Hiding while his comrades retreated, the straggler had plundered the camp and was waiting for the enemy in the hope that he would be allowed to retain his stolen goods. " Get out of this! " Sergeant Benson yelled, " Get out! " The laggard grumbled. Two sharpshooters grabbed him, forced him to buckle on his cartridge belt and pick up his rifle. He grabbed an armload of his treasures, but they were taken from his grasping hands. He responded lazily to orders and moved so slowly with the retreating force, all the while complaining in a pleading, whining voice, that Benson threatened to shoot him. But the sergeant could not execute the threat. He was tired of bloodshed. Instead he took a new pair of boots which the straggler wore and left him barefooted and empty-handed for the Federals.

Throughout the remainder of the day the retreat from Petersburg continued. Moving in single file, the dispirited soldiers walked on, not knowing their destination, shuffling along in hopeless flight, and a wave of Grant's men pushed behind them. The Confederates were too demoralized to fight; the officers were as ignorant of plans and as helpless as the enlisted men. As they marched the soldiers sang a Negro song borrowed from the Yankees.

> Ole Massa run away,
> De darky stay at home;
> I b'lieve in my soul dat the Kingdom am a comin';
> And de year ob Jubilo!

One soldier shot two pigs with one shot, or so he claimed, and the officers allowed a rest stop. Skinned and cleaned, the pigs were thrown into a pot of boiling water along with some cornmeal batter. The exhausted soldiers slept and awakened to find their meal and pork cooked almost to a jelly. As they wolfed their food, the sound of approaching troops sent the men scurrying behind trees. These troops were the first contingent of General James Longstreet's Corps in retreat from Richmond.

In that city, after breakfasting and reading reports on Sunday morning, Jefferson Davis departed for church. Wearing a dark suit, white shirt, and black tie, he left the Confederate White House and walked down Twelfth Street toward Capitol Square. Former Governor Francis R. Lubbock of Texas, a member of the executive staff, accompanied the President. Davis glanced at his polished but worn boots. He had ordered a new pair from Darby, Reed and Company, and delivery had been promised for Saturday evening, but tradesmen seldom kept their glib promises. Occasionally his tall, erect military bearing faltered as he stumbled in his stride, forgetting his near-blindness in one eye. He returned Sabbath greetings to men passing him, lifted his hat, and bowed to their wives.

As the two men neared the War Department office at ten-forty-five, Postmaster General Reagan rushed up to Davis. " Richmond must be evacuated," Reagan cried. Five minutes earlier, Lee had telegraphed that he could no longer hold his lines at Petersburg. He advised the abandonment of Richmond. Davis, Reagan, and Lubbock talked for a few minutes. Since the Postmaster General's news was not official and since Davis clung to form even in defeat, he decided to go on to church as he had planned. Moreover, in his deep religious conviction he needed the solace and strength which communion would supply. An evaluation of Lee's dispatch by Secretary of War Breckinridge or, better, a second and favorable report, might obviate immediate action, and if necessary an official messenger would bring the message to St. Paul's Episcopal Church.

Near St. Paul's on the corner of Grace and Ninth streets the sidewalks were filled with people. The warm clear day brought idlers to Capitol Square to bask in the morning sun. The haze of early morning had vanished in the sunshine that gave the city the pleasant radiance of early spring. No unusual sounds disturbed the Sabbath calm. Church bells rang with no hint of alarm in their melodious tones, and worshipers entered St. Paul's and other nearby churches in devout silence.

Davis took his pew and bowed in silent prayer. The congregation around him was mostly women, dressed in black, neat and clean in appearance and solemn in mien. Seated here and there were officers in uniform and a few elderly men dressed in dark blue or black suits which gleamed from repeated brushings and pressings. Dr. Charles Minnigerode, the rector, conducted the Episcopal service leading to monthly communion. In the solemnity of the church sounded the low pleasant voice of Minnigerode, the halting, ascending responses of the worshipers, and the clear tones of the choir. To many it seemed indeed that the house of the Lord was the very gateway to Heaven, and in their fullness of trust silent worshipers asked, " Can the Almighty forsake a people whose God is the Lord? " Constance Cary, later to be the wife of Burton H. Harrison, was seated behind the President, and she glanced at Davis's head and shoulders and probably wondered where her fiancé, the President's secretary, had gone with Mrs. Davis and the children. Emmie Crump, daughter of the Assistant Treasurer, demurely looked over the congregation to spot the President. Edward Hitchcock McDonald, on furlough and recuperating from typhoid fever, shifted restlessly in his pew. The choir sang " Jesus, Lover of My Soul," and the rector intoned, " The Lord is in His Holy Temple; let all the earth keep silence before Him! "

A military messenger eased through the church door and met the sexton for a whispered conversation. Mr. Irving, the pompous, well-groomed, and self-composed sexton of St. Paul's, walked down the middle aisle to Davis's pew and handed him a sealed envelope.[1] Carefully, silently Davis

---

[1] Emmie Crump, who was a Sunday School teacher and active member of St. Paul's, stated that Mr. Irving delivered the message to Davis. Other accounts differ. Most of them recall an officer in uniform approaching the President but others do not identify the messenger.

opened it and read what Reagan had told him before church. He reached for his hat, rose, and walked down the aisle with his usual quick military stride. A few people noticed the stern set of his lips and his calm face as he strode by. Some officers in uniform followed the President; and others, impatient, curious, or fearful, joined the exodus.

Most communicants, accustomed as they had become to calls for officials and officers, wondered at this variation which moved the President to leave, but they turned again to worship. Calmly Dr. Minnigerode continued the service. Alert observers saw him move to the side of the nave to accept and read a note. At the conclusion of communion he stepped forward to announce that by order of Brigadier General Richard S. Ewell the local defense forces would assemble that afternoon at three o'clock. This announcement became the subject of conversation as the congregation paused in exit on the columned portico of St. Paul's.

In other Richmond churches similar scenes occurred. General Samuel Cooper had been called from St. James to the War Department. At the Second Presbyterian Church the Reverend Moses Drury Hodge received a number of notices, and after each he motioned for a certain man to leave. The fourth request arrived while he read a hymn prior to its being sung, as was his custom (his communicants said he read with so much expression that its singing was an anticlimax), but this time his voice broke and he misread the words. Hodge could contain the dreadful news

---

Poetic and imaginative Carl Sandburg goes far afield in picturing an adjutant with muddy boots, a hard-riding man who pressed his sword to his side to silence it, striding up the aisle to hand Davis the message. It had not rained for two days, the streets of Richmond were dusty rather than muddy, and Lee's telegram came from the War Department office and not by messenger from the front at Petersburg. Of all those who recorded their recollections, Emmie Crump alone was active in the church and knew Sexton Irving and his insistence on form.

no longer. He told his congregation of the impending disaster and said that he feared that never again would they meet for worship. Richmond must fall to the Northern invaders. The quaver in his voice disappeared as Hodge warmed to his subject. In the eloquence for which he was noted he bade his congregation farewell and asked God to be merciful.

The news exploded with the force of a bomb. Members streamed from the church with no thought of predestination. Most of them remained silent, taking furtive glances at neighboring faces and returning each to his own dreadful thoughts. The news spread like wildfire over the city, but Richmond was swollen to a wartime population of almost one hundred thousand, even with the exodus of the past week, and many people did not learn of Lee's defeat for many hours.

AFTERNOON

IN THE MEANWHILE Jefferson Davis summoned his cabinet for its last meeting in Richmond. Benjamin came with his usual happy, jaunty air and pleasant smile. His mild Havana cigar and the very twirl of his slender, gold-headed cane gave the casual observer an impression of confidence such as that of the last man outside the ark who assured Noah that it would not be a hell of a shower after all. Breckinridge and Reagan walked from the War Office to the presidential suite in the old Customs Building. Though ill, Trenholm arrived also, and Mallory came from the Navy Department. For some unknown reason Attorney General Davis remained at his home. By presidential invitation Mayor Mayo, Governor Smith, and former Governor Letcher attended the meeting. Chief of Staff Samuel Cooper, along with other ranking chiefs of bureaus, stood ready to supply information or to relay decisions of the meeting to officers.

Davis reviewed the situation, read Lee's telegram, and admitted that immediate evacuation would cause the loss of many valuable archives and munitions. There would be insufficient time for packing and there was an inadequate number of trains. He had wired Lee about the possibility of holding his lines a little longer, but the General had responded emphatically. His Petersburg defenses could not be re-established, retreat could not be delayed beyond evening. Already the Petersburg railroad was under enemy fire and the Danville railway was endangered. Richmond must be evacuated. Governor Smith believed Lee would check Grant. The others were more realistic, but all hoped that Lee could unite his forces with those of General Joseph E. Johnston. The combined armies would defeat General William T. Sherman and in turn destroy Grant. Though Richmond must be abandoned, the government should remain a unit, with its officials and bureaus functioning at some other place, to direct the continued struggle.

Governmental archives presented no insurmountable problem. Reagan reported most of the post office records already shipped from Richmond. Other secretaries noted that their employees could destroy all valuable noncurrent records. Current and necessary archives could be boxed for shipment within twelve hours. Thousands of letters (especially of the Executive Department), treasury notes, bonds, and reports containing information of possible value to the enemy would be burned. Cabinet members accepted responsibility in directing their assistants to rush the packing and destruction. Secretary of the Navy Mallory's naval cadets on the training ship *Patrick Henry* were assigned the duty of guarding the gold and silver of the treasury. The almost half a million dollars of assets, the only money of value left to the Confederacy, together with the current archives, would be sent by wagons to the Danville Railroad station for loading on trains being held in readiness for movement.

Limited space on the trains determined other policy. The President, cabinet members, a few bureau chiefs and their key employees, Virginia state officials, and the necessary guards were given priority. Governor Smith declined the invitation to leave by train. He and some members of the Virginia legislature planned to go by the James River and Kanawha Canal to Lynchburg. Every man would be responsible for his own food and comfort. Danville was no more than eight hours away by a slow train. The Confederate government would be re-established in that city on Monday morning. The possibility that Federal cavalry might cut the Danville Railroad necessitated shipping mules and wagons on the presidential evacuation train, as well as horses for Davis and his cabinet. If necessary they would mount to escape capture.

The meeting ended. Davis returned to the executive mansion. Along the way anxious citizens stopped him repeatedly to ask for information. He told one lady that Lieutenant General William J. Hardee's force was only twelve miles away and might arrive in time to save Richmond. To others he admitted the necessity of evacuation but assured them that the government would return victorious. They responded with generous expressions of sympathy, for even the loss of Richmond was not too dear a price to pay for Southern independence. Finally he found privacy in the Confederate White House where, aided by his housekeeper and Negro butler, he packed the essentials for travel.

Back in departmental offices orders passed from secretary to assistant to clerk. Mallory and Breckinridge made lightning decisions. There was no time for written orders. Verbal commands passed from man to man. Trenholm dictated a letter for his treasurer John N. Henderson, which authorized him to have the records packed, to turn over to the first auditor for destruction all the old or mutilated issues of treasury notes, and to make all preparations for moving the Treasury Department to Danville. Despite his pain, the Secretary stopped to tell Emmie Crump that the President and cabinet would leave that night and that Northern occupation could be expected on Monday or Tuesday.

Nevertheless, Emmie tied on her bonnet and started for church to teach her regular afternoon Sunday School class. The relatively quiet streets of a few hours before were now filled with people of all economic classes. Friends told her there would be no school that day. Frightened by their pessimistic predictions, she hurried home to pack silver and other valuable household property. Mrs. Crump made a strong cotton belt, filled it with hoarded gold and silver coins, and tied it underneath her daughter's petticoats, hoping to keep it safe from marauding Yankees. Although her husband held an important Confederate post, he was absent on duty, and the family must remain in Richmond.

On the streets the rumors of Lee's defeat spread from corner to corner. At first a confident people could not believe evacuation necessary. Somehow, in some way, the invincible Lee would accomplish the impossible. In past years and months rumors about abandoning the city had spread with every call on the local defense forces and with every notice of an advancing enemy cavalry detachment. In time such reports had been proved false and Richmond had stood. And so it would be this time.

Yet the news irresistibly drew people from their homes. Some walked aimlessly. Two men meeting each other shook hands in silence and passed on with pale faces. Movement was everywhere, but there was no panic. Colorful Franklin Street, its spring flowers sending perfume from many gardens, was the rendezvous of friends. Diarist and "Rebel War Clerk" J. B. Jones met Judge Campbell on Ninth Street; the former justice was carrying a load of books under his arm and talking rapidly but inaudibly to himself. Jones hurried to the War Office where the rumors were confirmed as facts, and he was informed that all government employees with families were advised to remain in Richmond. On the street once more, he met James Lyons, who had no plan to flee although friends advised him to leave. Since Lyons was an original secessionist, they thought the Federals would hang him. Judge Campbell assured a friend that she would be safe in her rooms at the Spottswood Hotel and told her he was advising people to stay in their houses. She reported the conversation to the hotel manager, who immediately posted a notice urging his guests to remain. The energetic woman took to the streets again to carry the news to friends, but at the Pegram's, where a wife mourned her husband and a mother grieved for lost sons, the affliction was already so deep that the family expressed little concern for so small a matter as the loss of Richmond.

And so the hours dragged from noon until after two o'clock. Rumor met doubt, those who knew told the truth, but fact conquered fancy slowly. Individuals pointed to the increased number of wagons, driven in unusual haste, on the streets. Sunday activity in the departmental offices brought speculative comment, and men questioned soldiers as squads of local defense troops marched here and there to positions around government warehouses. Numbers of slaves stood silently in tight groups, listening and apprehensive, as bewildered as their masters. Members on their way to afternoon church services were informed that all meetings for afternoon and evening had been canceled; Lee was defeated, cabinet members were packing, and Richmond was doomed. These statements from reliable ministers passed from man to man, from slave to slave, from child to child. By the time the official announcement of evacuation was made, about three o'clock, few citizens doubted the fate of their city.

" Dismay reigned supreme," recalled a captain charged with special responsibility in the evacuation. Surrender had had no preparation, no rehearsal. The Confederacy was armed for defense, militarized to win, and it avoided even the whisper of action in defeat. So bewildered, stolid-faced people who asked what to do received no satisfactory answer. Some recalled the special message of Jefferson Davis to the Confederate Congress in February. He had assured the legislators then that the abandonment of Richmond would not end the Confederacy. The seat of government would be re-established elsewhere, the President had promised, and this reverse would stimulate renewed and successful effort. Recollections of his optimism gave little solace now, for they also brought to mind the forceful reply of the Richmond *Examiner*. " The evacuation of Richmond would be the loss of all respect and authority toward the Confederate Government, the disintegration of the army and the abandonment of the scheme of an independent Southern Confederation." What would be left, the *Examiner* continued, would be no more than a force for the protection of officials still persisting in keeping the Confederacy going. " The hope of establishing a Confederacy and securing its recognition among nations, would be gone forever." Comparing the two opinions, men accepted that of the *Examiner*. A fleeing government would doom itself to temporary stands, each succeeding one briefer than the previous one, until no authority or power remained anywhere. Likewise, if General Lee could not hold prepared positions with established supply lines, certainly retreat would not enable him to withstand the overwhelming power of Grant. Lee's defeat at Petersburg and the evacuation of Richmond would end the Confederacy.

Some people desired to serve to the last minute a cause already lost, while personal desire or fear motivated others. Duty bound the President, the cabinet members, and the military to continue the struggle. Realistic Judge Campbell saw the hopelessness of continued resistance and believed he could best serve the South by remaining in Richmond to plead lenient treatment from the conqueror. Many other leaders feared Northern vengeance. To the United States the war was rebellion, and a state seldom dealt kindly with defeated rebels. Tens of thousands of the unsuccessful had died for participation in European civil wars. The conviction of most Northerners that Southerners were guilty of treason foreshadowed attempts to punish the guilty. Few Southerners doubted the power of a victorious United States, and if might made right, prison or death lay ahead. Thus former rabid secessionists, state and Confederate officials, former federal office holders, and Confederate military officers were prime targets for retribution. Men with property or families in other areas of the South, visitors in Richmond, women who believed stories of Yankee atrocities, and soldiers who knew Northern prisons and were determined never to surrender again—all these sought means to leave the city.

Patients in the Confederacy's largest hospital on Chimborazo Heights overlooking the James River were determined not to be captured in their beds. The 150 buildings and 8,000 beds of Chimborazo Hospital had been filled with sick or wounded men, some of whom were accused of enjoying comfort after being restored to health. Thoughts of capture emptied most of the wards. Even men who could only crawl tried to escape, and one observer saw empty beds in which "paralysed, rheumatic, and helpless patients had laid for months." It almost seemed that by miracles the "lame, the halt, and the blind had been cured." Many patients were exchanged prisoners of war, and those too ill to leave were almost wild with the fear of again being made captives.

Former prisoner-of-war Leeland Hathaway swore he would not be captured and returned to a Northern prison camp. Disregarding orders of his physician, he and a friend walked and begged rides to get out of Richmond. On inquiry, Edward Hitchcock McDonald found that only those persons with passes would be allowed to leave on trains or government transports. Eight trains were scheduled to leave from the Danville station, but these trains and the canal boats were reserved for official use. At the War Department he waited to get a pass and transportation as a sick and furloughed soldier, but he never gained admission to an official who was empowered to sign permits. His cousin in the Navy Department told him that a horse and buggy would be sent out in charge of a departmental clerk. If McDonald would return at four, he might beg a ride in the buggy. McDonald did and got a seat, but the buggy was held back until all the soldiers crossed the bridge to Manchester. Throughout the afternoon and night McDonald and the clerk-driver waited for permission to move onto the bridge.

An ever increasing number of vehicles crowded the streets. Boxes, trunks, and packages were hastily loaded and driven to the Danville station by shouting, whip-wielding teamsters. Citizens determined to leave with the fugitive government looked on with amazement. Rumors of a possible sudden entry by Federal cavalry were told and made more frightful in the retelling. Only a few hours before skeptics discounted evacuation as a " Sunday sensation rumor "; now everyone accepted as fact the wildest talk. The stark, appalling reality of defeat immobilized the fearful.

It spurred others to act. Vehicles commanded any price in gold, silver, or United States currency. Two-horse and one-horse buggies and wagons, push carts, and wheelbarrows rented for ten, fifteen, twenty, and even a hundred dollars. Suddenly the streets were thronged with men seeking transportation; behind the men excited slaves carried trunks, boxes, and bundles of every size and description. A successful bidder for a vehicle, or at times a person who commandeered one at pistol point from an unfortunate free Negro, dumped his belongings into the conveyance and drove off at a furious rate. Throughout the heart of the city, wagons piled high with incongruous heaps of baggage intermingled with porters carrying huge loads. Wives and children wept and waved goodbye to husbands and fathers. People rode away from Richmond in all directions. Many of them discovered Mayo's Bridge closed to civilian traffic and followed country roads to nowhere other than the rural environs of Richmond. Some became discouraged by hours of aimless driving, or by broken axles, and returned to their homes.

Preparation for Federal occupation included the opening of banks. Constance Cary met the pale, wretched-looking president of one bank. Neither he nor the other officers of the institution, he told her, could guarantee any longer the safekeeping of money or household silver. By late afternoon owners of property stored in the vaults of the Traders, the Mechanics, and other banks had signed for their valuables. No one bothered to withdraw deposits of currency, and many people tossed aside Confederate bonds. Hoarded specie, Federal currency, household plate, stock certificates, and deeds were scooped into bags. At home the larger items were hidden or buried in back yards. Deeds, certificates, and coins were stuffed into pockets hastily made on petticoats. Cotton belts were stuffed with valuables and tied around feminine waists. At the banks, directors and clerks boxed specie and bullion for shipment. Gold and silver from Louisiana banks, sent to Richmond before the capture of New Orleans in 1862, were packed for still another trip. The total was not great in value. Millions of dollars in Confederate and state bills were dumped into the streets for burning. Thousand-dollar notes borne away by occasional gusts of wind were as ignored as they were worthless.

Behind closed doors women prepared their men for flight. Shirts, underwear, socks, ties, coats, trousers, together with little mementos of happier days, were pressed into valises. The activity helped to squeeze back tears. And from scant provisions, little packages of food, cooked or raw, were bundled and tied. Now terror penetrated every house. Yet women engaged in collecting and secreting their valuables or their cherished packets of letters bound with colorful ribbons took time to prepare some comforts for young bachelors. Few tears flowed; it was a time for action rather than weakness and sentiment. Grief was deep, but embraces were hasty and departures sudden.

Left alone or with their children, women sought protection in the houses of relatives or prepared meager meals for hungry broods. A faithful, honest Negro knocked at Constance Cary's door. A friend of hers at the Danville station had sent the servant with a ham and had paid him in Confederate currency. Constance took the unexpected gift and left for the security of her uncle's house. In another household two women tied on their homemade straw bonnets, trimmed with chicken feathers, gave themselves a last inspection, and joined the crowd in the streets. Rumor promised them free provisions at the Commissary Department. Amid the jostling crowd their courage fled. They found haven in the home of Colonel Walter Taylor's mother and requested the protection of Mrs. Taylor's young son, Bob, on their mission. But he could not go. The Colonel was to be married that day, Mrs. Taylor explained, and she needed Bob to complete arrangements. " Married! " the visitors exclaimed. " Sure," young Bob replied. " I took a message to Betty [Elizabeth Selden Saunders] this morning at church. Walter is coming in sometime this afternoon, and asked her to be ready. You know General Lee is moving and nobody knows where or for how long. If Betty is married to brother Walter, she can go with him." In their surprise the visitors forgot their purpose. It was well that they did, for the Commissary Department was not ready to open the doors of government warehouses.

Later, Colonel Taylor of General Lee's staff rode home to his fiancée. He stood in the Crenshaw house in dusty Confederate gray for the short marriage ceremony. With one embrace and a single kiss of promise, he rode back to duty. Plans for the bride to live near the front disappeared with the necessity for speedy retreat. Betty waved to her departing groom and wondered in how many days, if ever, he would return.

Across the street two spectators of the marriage turned from the window to their drab one-room abode. Their store of provisions was larger that day than that of most of Richmond's citizens. Two bags of rice, one of dried peas, two firkins of butter, an almost empty bag of potatoes, and some dried apples lay in one corner of the room; almost a ton of coal and a small pile of wood cluttered another; a frying pan, pots, and other utensils were on the hearth; and personal belongings loaded the bed, wardrobe, and bureau. Neither despaired. Their faith in Lee and his ragged army amounted to superstition. One woman poked the fire under a pot of rice, while the other prepared some peas and dried apples.

Not far away Elizabeth Van Lew studied humanity in crisis. She saw cavalry and infantrymen bidding friends and relatives farewell. Facial expressions told her the soldiers wanted to stay but felt they must go, and she noted that individual will knew only obedience in the army. Seeing a neighbor on the steps next door, Miss Van Lew went over to visit. Children, and even adults, called her " Crazy Bet " and justly accused her of Union sympathies, of harboring escaped Federal prisoners, and of spying for the enemy. Often neighbors had ostracized her, but now the times were askew. She commented on the defeat of Lee and the possibilities of peace, but only the evacuation of Richmond interested the neighbor.

"The war will end now," Crazy Bet said. "The young men's lives will be saved."

"I have a son in the army about Petersburg," the neighbor replied.

"There is hope for his life now," Elizabeth assured her companion. "Peace will end those terrible words 'the last man must die,' which are so often spoken and acted upon."

"It would be better for all to die," was the response. "Anything would be better than to fall under the United States again."

Sadly Crazy Bet rose, returned to her own doorstep, and pondered the definition of insanity.

Miles away from the imposing Van Lew mansion, Miss Emma Mordecai considered her situation at Rosewood Plantation more precarious even than that of people living in Richmond. Other than a few servants, her household included her sister-in-law, the ill, frail Rosina (Mrs. Augustus Mordecai) and the latter's attractive daughter, Augusta. Although the city limits were near, no neighbors lived within call. Augusta knew she could not defend herself against lustful Northern soldiers. The thought of uniformed Negro Yankees made her shudder. Two Sunday visitors at the plantation were set on returning to Richmond. Caroline, a cousin and one of the visitors, urged Augusta to go with them, but she feared to remain with her mother and was even more afraid of separation. Emma walked a mile with Caroline and confessed that her faith in God was insufficient to erase dread of the insult, injury, and outrage in store for three women on a lonely farm.

Caroline returned to tumult. Sounds of hammers and saws floated from governmental department and bureau offices. Almost half a million worth of specie, gold and silver bullion, gold plate and jewelry (contributed within the past months by patriotic Virginians), Mexican silver pesos, and coins of other countries were nailed up in boxes or packed in sturdy trunks. Guards walked by the sides and rear of the wagon carting the treasury to the Danville station. There sixty naval cadets from the training ship *Patrick Henry* (under command of Captain William Parker), resplendent in their clean uniforms, packed the valuables into a boxcar standing outside the depot on Fourteenth Street. Then disciplined, erect, and serious, they stood guard as other wagons and carts arrived with archives and supplies.

At the station Captain Peter Helms Mayo had trains waiting. For two days he had supervised troop and supply movements from the depot of the Richmond and Petersburg line. Early Sunday afternoon Quartermaster Alexander Robert Lawton instructed Mayo to prepare a special train at the Danville station for the President, cabinet members, their personal effects, and, in case of need, horses for the officials. Mayo was also ordered to make up other trains, using all available engines and cars, for the transport of archives and supplies.

During the past week, cars and engines of the Danville road had been operated at more than 100 per cent of rated capacity. Since the railroad ran fairly near Petersburg, it had been used to supplement the Richmond and Petersburg line. Most of its rolling stock was in service. Now the evacuation of Petersburg made the road to that city useless. However, engines could not be moved quickly from one line to another. The transfer of equipment from one station to the other was a major and time-consuming operation. There was not enough time to do it on that Sunday. Moreover, the train crews were scattered in their homes throughout the city with no expectation of an emergency call. Repeated, shrill whistles of the old yard engine, a prearranged signal, called the trainmen to work. Before six o'clock the most comfortable coach in the yard, boxcars, horsecars, and the best available engine were made ready for the presidential party. Other trains were made up, with fires in the engines and steam in the boilers, to receive the effects of the government.

This activity at the station continued as the retreating troops of Longstreet's Corps began to leave the city. The first soldiers marched through the streets in perfect order, but lacking their former animation as when on maneuvers and passing through Richmond. Yet most civilians were proud of the uniformed men as they marched out on their hopeless retreat. Hats came off in salute; some women sobbed, others whispered, " God bless and speed you." Successive waves of soldiers seemed to bring more dispirited and listless men. Clifford Dowdey pictured them shuffling up Main Street hill past the American Hotel. Several ladies watched from the hotel's iron-grilled balcony. One young girl waved her delicate handkerchief in the old familiar greeting which had always brought a cheer. Not one soldier acknowledged her tribute to valor. Her arm froze, then fell limply to her side, and her face paled with embarrassment and pain. Wagons crowded past the infantry, breaking formations, jostling the soldiers as though announcing that now supplies and archives were of more importance than men.

EVENING

AT THE CONFEDERATE White House Jefferson Davis gave his housekeeper final instructions for closing his home of almost four years. He fingered mementos and bric-a-brac which his wife Varina had collected and enjoyed. She had been unable to take them with her, and there was no room for them now in his bags. Aides helped him pack coats, waistcoats, and trousers. A dressing robe, towels, razor and strop, comb, brush, and toothbrush went into a small dressing case for his toilet. Linen shirts, ties, underwear, shoes, and extra shoelaces joined the suits and almost filled the large valise. He wrapped eyeglasses and placed them near envelopes and notepaper. Four pistols and a case of ammunition indicated his determination to fight for his life. At the last minute he added a picture of his wife and himself, and one of General Lee.

By seven o'clock the President reached the Danville station. The naval cadets saluted, and Breckinridge led him to a seat in the coach. One by one the cabinet members arrived. Judah Benjamin puffed his cigar, ignoring the danger of fire in the littered station. Supported by his wife Anna, Secretary of the Treasury Trenholm entered the car and, exhausted, lay cramped on a narrow seat. A shot of morphine eased his pain, but he moved only to change position and did not leave the coach. Postmaster General Reagan walked impatiently up and down the platform. Naval Secretary Mallory joined him from time to time. Attorney General Davis remained calm and unobtrusive. Breckinridge rode his horse along the cars as though giving them a final inspection. In all some thirty men and Anna Trenholm crowded into the coach and awaited the signal to move out of the station.

Minutes mounted into hours, but the train remained motionless. Jefferson Davis left his seat to confer with Breckinridge. Reagan found a stick, whittled it intently to the rhythm of his chewing tobacco, and meditated in evident perplexity. Within the station, and around it, some people were bidding friends Godspeed; other people vainly tried to obtain places on the train. The crew and the hissing old engine were ready. The impatient passengers were puzzled, then became worried. Some said the baggage was not loaded, but there was no activity on the platform near the baggage cars. Horses whinnied and stamped in fright in their boxcar. Actually Davis and Breckinridge were responsible for the delay. They hoped that good news from General Lee would cancel the need for flight. Timing already had reached the critical point. Federal cavalry might seize a section of the Danville road, might capture the treasury and archives, and might force the President and his cabinet to seek safety on horseback.

Captain William Parker approached Breckinridge with a request. Stacked in the station were bales of blankets and clothing, boxes of shoes, piles of saddles, and other scarce commodities. Two trainloads had been unloaded there that morning for transfer to the Richmond and Petersburg station. The naval cadets had no blankets, and Parker asked permission to open some of the bales to outfit his men. Inside the station Breckinridge was appalled at the store of goods. He knew Lee's army had been in critical need for weeks. Peter Helms Mayo explained that the arrival of many trains from the south had overtaxed dray facilities between the Danville and Petersburg stations. Then news of the defeat at Petersburg had ended transfers to the now useless Petersburg line. Obviously Lee could use the supplies, but his line of retreat was unknown; even if officials knew any place to ship the material to prevent its capture, there were no more boxcars nor engines. All available wagons were being loaded, but these could transport only a fraction of the stores. Breckinridge agreed that nothing could be done to save the material. He directed Parker to take everything his men needed, and the cadets eventually boarded the train loaded with valuables.

While the heads of the Confederate government waited, state and local officials conferred. At nine o'clock members of the Virginia legislature assembled in the gaslit halls of the statehouse. The lawmakers had been meeting every day since March 29, and each day promptly adjourning for lack of a quorum. On Sunday evening the legislators considered no bills and passed no resolutions. They met, they talked, and most of them agreed to escape by boat on the canal. Governor " Extra Billy " Smith said he would leave on horseback and follow the canal route to Lynchburg. In that city he planned to establish a temporary capital and bring the cadets of the Virginia Military Institute from Lexington to defend it.

The burden of continued government fell then to city authorities. The council had met during the afternoon to discuss the surrender; but Governor Smith, who met with the councilmen, convinced many of them that Lee would reestablish his lines. Therefore little planning had been done. When Mayor Mayo called the council into session in the evening, there was no longer doubt of the necessity for planning an evacuation. The Mayor knew that General Ewell had orders to destroy Confederate commissary stores and tobacco to prevent their falling to the Federals. The artillery, infantry, and picket guards were scheduled to leave Richmond about three o'clock in the morning. A cavalry detachment would scour the city for stragglers and protect the engineers charged with burning the James River bridges. Although exact hours could not be predicted, there would surely be some time between the disappearance of the Confederate and arrival of the Federal soldiers.

This period of emptiness worried the councilmen. Richmond's forty-man police force would not be able to keep order in the city. In past weeks lethargy had prevented the organization of a volunteer force, and it was now too late to deputize a citizen patrol. The Nineteenth Virginia Militia would operate from Capitol Square, but the number of its men was small and their physical condition poor. In the unprotected city, fires might break out at any time, but the fire department had neither the men nor the equipment to handle more than a small blaze. On one action the council agreed—people filled with whiskey could bring on riot and anarchy. Although liquor was officially banned, an ample supply of illegal barrels was hidden in dives and in respectable clubs throughout the city. An ordinance authorized destruction of all intoxicating beverages. Each councilman was charged with organizing a committee in his ward to find and break open barrels and kegs, and to pour out the contents. Policemen would protect the committee, and records would be made of the destruction so that owners could later claim compensation for the supplies destroyed.

At the moment of adjournment a councilman asked about the surrender of Richmond. What protocol should be observed? No one knew exactly, never before having experienced defeat, but all agreed that it should be done. Formal surrender by the mayor might appease the conqueror and mitigate the rigors of occupation. The council authorized Mayor Mayo to ride out at daylight and deliver Richmond to the Federal commander.

In the outlying defenses of the city, Confederate bands covered the retreat with a military concert. Federal musicians responded to Confederate tunes with national airs until the night was filled with melody.

Neither Confederate soldier nor officer knew the exact reason for retreat. That afternoon rumors had been spread of a serious reverse at Hatcher's Run and of the necessity for abandoning both Petersburg and Richmond. Detachments pulled out of the defense works around Richmond from time to time, and full retreat began around ten o'clock. Other than the route through the city and over Mayo's

Bridge to Manchester, no soldier knew where he was headed. Thousands of troops began the march with empty haversacks and little in their stomachs. Near midnight they entered and passed through Richmond.

The steady and continuous tramp of troops, the rumble of ordnance, artillery, and supply wagons filled the main streets. Soldiers who were determined to follow the Stars and Bars to the end marched rapidly across the bridge with a firm tread, but sadly and silently they bade farewell forever to the Confederate capitol. However, many turned from the ranks at dark corners to hide in the night. Escape came easy for these stragglers in a city of confusion.

The long, low street wagons of the quartermaster's department rattled over rough pavements. Boys and Negroes called them " Jeff Davis's musical boxes." Apparently they were built to get the maximum noise from a given amount of wood and iron. Every piece of timber, every screw and bolt that held the pieces together, seemed to have an average play of two inches, and as the wagons moved along the streets they made an uproar equal to the rolling of a thousand barrels of rock down a steep hill. These wagons, together with privately owned buggies, drays, and carts, covered the quick desertion of thousands of tired, disheartened soldiers.

Hidden by the night and fearful of the day, friend called on friend. A mecca was the home of Moses Hodge, the popular pastor of the Second Presbyterian Church. His house on the northeast corner of Fifth and Main streets was in the line of retreat. For more than three years the friendly minister, his wife Susan, and especially the five girls who lived with them, had attracted officers and enlisted men. So frequent were the visitors on Sunday evening that young Addison Hodge, a nephew of the preacher, was kept busy opening and closing the front door. Some soldiers stopped to thank Susan Hodge and Lizzie Brown, wife of the editor of the *Central Presbyterian*, for their visits and gentle care given in Richmond hospitals. Others wished to say farewell to the girls. Members of Hodge's congregation came for spiritual uplift to meet the coming day.

Similar scenes occurred at the homes of other ministers and at residences of the socially elite. Fearing the morning, relative found comfort in relative and friend in friend. Courtesy demanded inquiry about Uncle John or Cousin Robert, the time of their departure, and where they were going. Woman speculated with woman about the Yankees. With so few Southern men left in Richmond, ladies must protect themselves. Owners exchanged praise of faithful slaves. But as the hours languished, visitors departed. Near midnight the Hodge family went upstairs to bed, leaving the nephew awake in the parlor to greet late-comers or to receive messages. Addison Hodge gazed through the window toward the James River and the soldiers marching across Mayo's Bridge.

The stream of wagons and moving men lessened in number. Hundreds of soldiers remained in the city to hunt stragglers or to guard public buildings. Union prisoners from the notorious Libby Prison were being rushed south for exchange. In their haste guards forgot to take paroles of five hundred of the seven hundred prisoners who were on the steamer *Cossack* headed for Fortress Monroe near the mouth of the James River. Other Federal prisoners of war, not knowing how close they were to freedom, escaped into the night. Some of them wandered through the streets to be welcomed and hidden by Elizabeth Van Lew. Wagons and men continued to move, but the pace and numbers decreased, and the noise abated. Bands ceased their serenades in the outlying defense works. Silence brooded over the contending battle lines. Confederate musicians joined their fellows in retreat; only picket guards remained within the battlements.

In the last minutes of April 2 a few men rushed to the Danville station. General Josiah Gorgas, Confederate ordnance chief, finished all he could do in helping his wife Amelia move to her daughter's residence. After making sure of a wagon for the following morning to complete the moving, Gorgas left his wife standing guard over the remaining household goods. Wounded George Alexander Martin rose from his bed at the last minute, pulled on his gray uniform, and walked to the Danville station. There, after a tedious and painful wait, he found space on a flatcar. He lay on the boards with nothing beneath him, and above him the great vault of Heaven seemed " ready to receive in its folds, the devoted band of patriots, who, for four years, had struggled under its canopy."

Martin failed to note in his diary the presence of the presidential train. To this day the time of its departure remains a question.[2] Breckinridge had alternated between conferring with Davis and riding around the station area. Anna Trenholm comforted her husband, and probably in her impatience to be moving to any destination where she could find a bed for her sick man, she watched the minutes drag by more carefully than others did. Benjamin covered his impatience by smiling underneath his curly black beard. Mallory's normally red face became more florid. Apparently Davis remained unperturbed by the possibility of capture en route to Danville. From time to time he shook cinders from his Confederate-gray waistcoat and trousers, brushed his graying beard, or lifted his wide-brimmed felt hat to pat his well-groomed hair.

[2] In her diary Anna Trenholm gave the hour as eleven that night and the time of arrival in Danville as five in the morning. John H. Reagan recalled that it was near midnight before the train began to move. Peter Helms Mayo, who was in charge of trains, gave nine o'clock as the hour. In articles for their newspapers, correspondents fixed the departure at various times between seven o'clock and midnight.

Just before its departure, families and wounded veterans begged passage on the train. A few families crowded into boxcars, leaving their baggage on the station platform. Some of Gorgas' ordnance workers climbed aboard, and veterans found room on a flatcar and on roofs of boxcars. Captain Parker's cadets took their places for guard duty. Breckinridge, who did not plan to leave Richmond by train, held the bridle of his large, sleek horse for a final word at the coach window with Davis. The decrepit engine jerked and slowly pulled the overcrowded old cars out of the station on treacherous rails.

Minutes later the train moved carefully onto the river bridge. Looking out, the passengers saw the traffic on Mayo's Bridge, but darkness covered the movement of men piling wood on it and pouring turpentine to speed the fires soon to be lighted. On reaching the south bank of the James, the engineer pulled the whistle cord. The shrill blast floated back in salute to the doomed capital of the Confederacy and drifted out to Rosewood, where Emma Mordecai lay sleepless and young Augusta pressed her fear of the morning against her mother's breast.

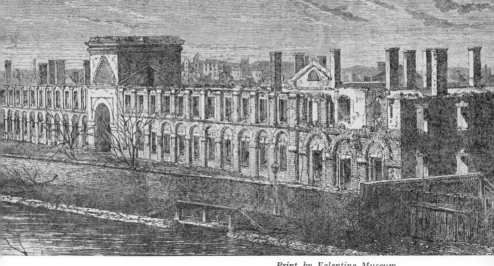

Print by Valentine Museum

(*II*)

THE DAY THAT RICHMOND FELL
April 3, 1865

MIDNIGHT PASSED UNNOTICED in the current of activity
that flowed through Richmond. The rush of fugitives carried
from one day into the next, and preparations for the surrender of the city began. One activity abated while the other
increased. Clerks in governmental offices continued dumping
letters, documents, and records into the streets. Firelight
from the burning papers flickered on walls; in the dim light
shadows of workers, running to and fro, climbed buildings or
lengthened into darkness on the streets. In the calm night
smoke flowed upward, drifted outward in thick layers, and
yawned over the city. Thousands of stars and a descending
moon cast their pale light.

Here and there loaded or empty wagons creaked and rumbled through the streets. The noise neither aroused sleepers nor disturbed the thoughts of those who rolled and tossed in their beds. Anita Dwyer Withers, a visitor from Texas, later recalled that her fright, anxiety, and dread during the night made her ill for a week afterward. For Emma Mordecai every hour was a day, as she slept, awakened, dozed, and roused; every unrecognizable sound made her tremble; and the whistle of engines and the clank of cars on the Danville Railroad brought her questions about the coming day. Peter Helms Mayo completed his work at the Danville station shortly after one o'clock in the morning. He walked to his small house on Grace, between Third and Fourth streets, held his wife and kissed her tear-drenched face, patted the upturned bottom of his sleeping infant daughter, said goodbye to his sister, and left to escape by Mayo's Bridge. Marcia Bayne walked hand in hand with her father Josiah Gorgas toward the railroad depot. At one of the gates to the arsenal he admonished a guard on the danger of fire. Father and daughter moved on in the dark. A little after one his train pulled out of the station, but two hours later it was still on the south side of the James River in Manchester.

Gorgas feared the destruction of Richmond. On Saturday he had protested the plan of General Ewell to burn the warehouses in event of evacuation and had suggested that barrels of turpentine could be poured over tobacco to destroy its value to the Yankees. But his proposal had been rejected. He had overheard Secretary Breckinridge order the firing of all the James River bridges, and he knew that sparks from such fires could ignite the arsenal.

Mayor Mayo and other citizens of Richmond also protested the plan to burn Confederate warehouses. James D. Scott headed a committee that was formed to confer with

Ewell. Major Samuel W. Melton, one of a large number of adjutant and inspector generals charged with supervising the destruction of stores, met the committee but refused to heed its protest. He emphatically denied that burning the warehouses would endanger Richmond and characterized a contrary statement " as a cowardly pretext on the part of citizens, trumped up to endeavor to save their property for the Yankees." Some merchants received even blunter treatment from Secretary Breckinridge, who reputedly told them " he didn't care a damn if every house in Richmond was consumed, *the Warehouses must be burned.*" After the crisis no one would be able to place responsibility for burning the stores.[1] The laws of the Confederacy allowed commanders no

[1] Reporters of the Philadelphia *Press* (April 7) and the Baltimore *Clipper* (April 5) talked with citizens who blamed Breckinridge. The *New York Times* correspondent wrote that it was not General Lee, but Jefferson Davis and his secretary of war who were responsible. An article in the Richmond *Times* (April 21) blamed Major Melton. The Baltimore *Clipper* (April 8) claimed that Breckinridge joined the citizens in protest, but that Ewell refused to reconsider. The Richmond *Whig* (April 14) stated that Ewell and Major I. H. Carrington opposed burning the warehouses, but that Breckinridge overruled them. Ewell later denied responsibility and stated that the citizens protested to Davis early in the evening of April 2, but that the President condemned them and that Major Melton echoed Davis's words to another committee. Ewell claimed that he warned the city authorities of danger because of a brisk wind which was blowing from the south. The fact that it was calm until after sunrise on April 3 discredits Ewell's reminiscences.

In February Ewell had received orders from General Lee, along with a copy of the Confederate statute, both requiring the burning of tobacco and cotton to prevent their capture by the enemy. Ewell advised Mayor Mayo, merchants, and warehouse owners of his orders. He and Scott inspected warehouses containing the commodities, and after consultation with the city council, concluded that the storehouse could be burned without endangering the city. The General refused an offer from the Ordnance Department of barrels of turpentine to

discretion. Supplies, especially cotton and tobacco, must be burned or otherwise destroyed to prevent their capture by Federal forces. Evidently neither officials nor citizens dared to protest this established " scorched earth policy " on the ground that the war was over and any tobacco and cotton which the United States might gain did not justify the possible burning of Richmond. Some citizens considered resistance, but the Confederate military controlled the city.

The decision stood to burn four warehouses: the Public Warehouse near the Petersburg railroad depot, Shockoe Warehouse in the center of the business district close to the Gallego flour mills, and Mayo's and Dibrell's warehouses on Cary Street would all be fired before complete evacuation of the Confederate troops. The still atmosphere lessened the possibility of the fire spreading to other buildings. Fires would not be lighted until every available wagon was filled with stores from the Confederate warehouses and on its way to Lee's retreating army.

Preparation for other destruction was hastened. Sailors on the nine gunboats anchored in the river packed them with explosives. Kegs of powder, shells, and cartridges filled the magazines of three ironclads (the *Virginia*, the *Richmond*, and the *Fredericksburg*) and six wooden ships (the *Nansemond*, the *Hampton*, the *Roanoke*, the *Torpedo*, the *Shrapnel*, and the *Patrick Henry*). Before dawn engineers attached fuses to these ships, which were now floating powder boxes. All the vessels combined carried only seventeen guns. Neither the cannon nor the ships themselves would have been real additions to the powerful Northern navy. But even more senseless was the plan to explode the powder magazine. It

---

speed the fire, fearing the intensity of the blaze would endanger other buildings. He warned Mayor Mayo of the danger from plunderers and urged the city council to organize a voluntary police force. The Mayor tried to follow this suggestion, but only one man volunteered.

stood near the heart of Richmond, but in a ravine whose sloping hills might absorb the force of the explosion. Only the almshouse buildings lay near the magazine, and warning was given to the poverty-stricken residents. They fled from their beds in night clothes and stayed for hours on open ground behind a hill. Confederate ships could be displayed as souvenirs of war and wounded pride might explain the destruction of the gunboats, but the United States possessed abundant supplies of powder. The gain from destroying the ammunition in the Richmond magazine could never justify the danger to the city.

Governor Smith participated in none of the post-midnight decisions. About one o'clock he left his wife, daughter, and two of their friends at the governor's mansion and rode to the James River and Kanawha Canal. There he remained until the last boat departed. With an aide and a Negro servant he rode along the towpath toward Lynchburg. At a break in the path his horse stumbled and fell into the canal. "Extra Billy" jumped clear of the saddle, but fell underneath the rearing and struggling horse. He escaped from this double jeopardy of drowning and flailing hoofs, remounted, and rode on wet, bruised, and hatless. More than a day later his attempts to organize a force in Lynchburg failed. He made patriotic appeals, addressing every gathering and urging men to join the army, but he met with silence or argument. Finally he ended his stay by " damning such a miserable set " and rode away to join the fleeing Confederate cabinet.

Back in Richmond the committees that were organized to destroy whiskey mapped their action. Retreating soldiers continued to cross the bridges to Manchester. As the traffic lightened, guards prepared to fire the railroad trestles. Mayo's Bridge would remain until the last minute. Then engineers, protected by a cavalry detachment, would light piles of turpentine-drenched wood stacked on the bridge.

In addition to soldiers and teamsters, other men roamed the streets. Two escaped Federal prisoners knocked at Miss Van Lew's door. Because of threats to burn her house, she was standing guard, moving in the dark from room to room. She welcomed the fugitives, and others who came later, but warned them to light no candles or lamps. The prisoners had escaped as the guards marching them south had relaxed. One of them, a woman accused of being a spy, told Miss Van Lew that she had walked thirty-two miles along country roads, mostly at night, to reach Richmond. Other prisoners had pressed against buildings while moving cautiously in the direction of their Federal comrades. Care was necessary, for more and more sleepless men of Richmond were leaving their houses to roam the streets or to watch the retreating army.

Suddenly, shortly before dawn, terrific explosions shook the city. One after another the ironclads with their loaded magazines vanished in a fury of spray and noise. Buildings quivered, windows rattled and shattered as far away as two miles from the river. Emmie Crump jumped from her bed, dazed, and could not comprehend awakening in the middle of the living room. Broken glass lay all around her. She and other frightened women thought the Federals were shelling the city. Then another and louder blast resounded as the powder magazine went up in fire, smoke, and dust.

The magazine was a small brick building, twenty by thirty feet, twenty feet high, covered with a steep slate roof. A thick brick wall some six feet high and six feet from the main building surrounded the magazine. It lay against the slope of a hill almost a hundred yards from Shockoe Hill Cemetery and the same distance from the almshouse buildings which housed the paupers of the city. The force of the explosion spread out in four waves. One wrecked the almshouses, totally demolishing the smaller buildings and destroying half the main one. A second wave moved westward and uphill to level the northern wall of the cemetery. The other two explosive waves expended themselves harmlessly against nearby hills. " Nothing but a long narrow trench in the ground, looking like a grave of a resurrected giant, marked the spot where the magazine stood." Bricks were powdered into fine dust as if they had passed through a gristmill. No rubbish fell back into the holes of the foundations, but spread outward over the green hills in four lanes, covering the grass with a reddish powder. Some bricks were thrown as far as Second Street. One passed through the roof of a small house on Second Street and struck an aged Negro in the temple, instantly killing him. Most of the glass in the city hospital and the new poorhouse was shattered. Had the magazine not been in a small ravine, the loss of life would have been appalling.

As it was, eleven paupers died. After the residents of the almshouse had heeded warnings by scurrying behind a hill, their impatience had grown with their discomfort. Night dress did not protect old bodies from the cool morning air. The more courageous or the colder went back for clothing and blankets. Some were in the buildings while others were mounting steps to their verandas when the blast came. They never heard it. Those on the steps were hurled against walls, and falling roofs crushed those within the buildings.

The explosions filled the streets with people. From hovels of the poor and from houses of the wealthy men rushed out to investigate. Negroes free and slave, Irishmen, Anglo-Saxons crowded into the streets. Most women of the upper strata of society remained indoors, but others had no inhibitions. Then soldiers fired two of the bridges, and mounting flames lighted the river front. At street corners unnamed individuals shouted welcome news: food and clothing would be distributed from the government warehouses.

Men grabbed carts and wheelbarrows, women snatched up tubs and pots and joined the empty-handed running madly to Public, Shockoe, Mayo, and Dibrell warehouses. Scenting opportunity, stragglers and deserters from the Confederate army came out of hiding to swell the crowd.

It was not yet a mob. Some members of the moving mass could still be diverted, and were, by the sight of committee-men entering buildings and rolling out barrels and kegs of whiskey, knocking in their heads, and pouring the fiery liquid into gutters. Many poor people of Richmond suffered every day from hunger, but for months and even years they had tasted no liquor. Women dipped their pots into the dirty flow and lifted them to receptive lips. Men grabbed half-empty kegs and drank. Sons of Gideon lay prone and lapped the flowing streams or in passing scooped the liquid by hand from gutter to mouth. Both men and women, white and colored, pushed, shoved, and heaved their way to sources of supply.

Some members of the crowd remained to drink again and again, but others drank quickly and rushed on to the warehouses. There Confederate soldiers still guarded those who were loading wagons. The liquor was working in empty stomachs; soon it would give unaccustomed courage to timid souls. The crowd watched the loading in sullen silence.

Prisoners in the state penitentiary, awakened by the explosions, milled about in their cells. Passers-by stopped on the west side of the building to yell news of defeat and evacuation. The prisoners shouted for guards and release, they pounded floors, and one burly man forced the door of his cell. He dashed downstairs, returned with an axe, and knocked open three or four doors. The liberated prisoners frightened the guards, who dropped their keys and ran. Within ten minutes every prisoner was free. They plundered the prison storehouse. The lucky ones shed their distinctive garb for stolen civilian clothes, while others ransacked nearby houses to find more. They fired the prison workshop and then roamed the streets like fierce, ferocious beasts searching for food and valuable property.

After workmen had loaded the last wagon at Shockoe Warehouse, quantities of hams, bacon, flour, and meal remained. Quartermaster officers ordered the guards to join their retreating comrades and invited the civilians to help themselves. Hundreds of shouting men and women, black and white, surged forward. They pushed and shoved their way into the storerooms. Individuals who had not eaten a good meal in months stopped to gape at the stores of meat, cereals, sugar, and coffee. This momentary pause soon broke into feverish acquisition. With eager hands and overloaded arms, the first entrants bucked the incoming mass to find the street, to deposit their gains there, and to return to the warehouse for more. Rolling barrels of flour cut swaths through milling people. Sacks broke, barrels split, and hundreds of trampling feet sank into the soft flour and meal. Upstairs in the warehouse commissary agents knocked in kegs of whiskey and poured their contents from windows. Extended tubs, buckets, and pans caught the descending liquor. Men without containers held out their hats while others pulled off their boots to catch the rare liquor. Not yet had the crowd become an hysterical mob. Its main purpose was still food for hungry families. But most of the liquor was consumed immediately, and its effect came with dramatic swiftness.

FIRE AND RIOT

THE COMMISSARY AGENTS dumped the last of the whiskey and prepared to burn Shockoe Warehouse. Before they lighted torches, a civilian fired a canal boat loaded with bacon, which floated at the dock near Mayo's Bridge. Sparks from the canal boat ignited two nearby boats; these swung under the bridge and set it ablaze. Guards pulled the ships away and doused the lower superstructure of the bridge to extinguish the flames.

This unexpected threat to the one remaining escape route to Manchester triggered the planned fires. While people snatched provisions in Shockoe, its store of tobacco was ignited. Ignoring the plunderers at other warehouses and at the Danville station, soldiers applied the torch at those places. A squad drove away a group of Frenchmen protecting their nation's tobacco at DeVoss's Warehouse and fired that one. Other soldiers set fire to privately owned storehouses along the river front. Flares in hand, they moved to the Tredegar iron mill, but its owner, General Joseph R. Anderson, met them with an armed force of workmen who saved the South's largest iron works. Near seven o'clock the last regular troops crossed Mayo's Bridge.

The Seventh South Carolina cavalry, assigned the task of rounding up stragglers, cut short their work because of the rapid advance of Federal troops. As they spurred their horses through Rockett's—a suburb of shacks—workingmen's families of bold and dirty women, dirtier children, and scowling old men lined the sidewalks. Their number was relatively small, for most people were at the burning warehouses. One buxom Irish woman stood on the pavement's edge with her arms folded, an expression of intense scorn on her face, and yelled in her brogue, "After four years of fighting, yo're running like dawgs." On reaching Main Street the cavalrymen guided their mounts through a motley crowd—bareheaded women, their arms filled with goods of every description, their hair hanging unkempt about their ears; people rushing to unload their gains; and a current of the empty-handed surging in the opposite direction toward the source of plunder. All around the crowds were the roaring and crackling of flames, the snorting of horses, the trampling of hoofs on pavement. From above everything the red sun came dimly through the cloud of smoke which now hung like a pall over the city.

The soldiers pushed their horses up Main Street. Near Twenty-Second Street the flames swept across Main, and the cavalry turned right to get above them on Franklin Street. After skirting the burning squares, the detachments turned back to Main. A smaller bridge across the canal near the James River was in flames, but not the larger one. At this point the pillagers almost blocked the street with their loot from the warehouses. Cavalryman Edward M. Boykin saw a white man and woman fighting over a barrel of flour. The man raised his arm to strike the woman, but a stout Negro drove the white man away by threatening to throw him into the canal.

The cavalry crossed the bridge at the south end of Fourteenth Street and scattered lighted faggots to burn the structure behind them. William J. Brown and Robert Allen ran onto the bridge to fight the flames. Before they could make headway, shots drove them away. After this last act the soldiers sped over the bridge and left it burning from end to end.

Secretary Breckinridge joined the cavalrymen in Manchester as they turned to look back across the James at Richmond. There, too, Peter Helms Mayo and the newly married Walter Taylor gazed at the burning city. Mayo saw the flames and smoke rising from the Danville station where he had spent most of the past few days as supervisor of transportation. Taylor vainly sought the Crenshaw house where his virgin wife was staying. All of them gasped to see the smoke rolling rapidly toward the center of Richmond. It seemed that the heat created its own breeze, which blew from the southeast. Then the smoke hid Richmond, and the three watchers rode away.

Hot currents of air from the leaping flames lifted burning fragments aloft and, carried by the wind, they dropped on distant roofs. The hungry fire spread from building to building toward Main Street and on beyond. The few volunteer firemen who responded to calls found every firehose chopped into pieces. Richmond was aflame.

Edward M. Boykin estimated that 5,000 deserters remained in the city. These potentially dangerous men joined hundreds of thieves, flimflam artists, and shady characters of both sexes who lived under the shadow of the law. More than 350 convicts had broken out of the penitentiary and roamed the streets without fear of capture. Thousands of men, women, and children from Rockett's and other slum areas searched for food. Ordinarily they were law-abiding citizens, their poverty in life made endurable by visions of plenty in Heaven. They worked hard at times, lived boisterously when circumstances permitted, and by attending church on Sunday accumulated assets in the hereafter. For many years their lot had been one of repeated hardship. Their loved but often mistreated children cried from hunger and cold, those little delicacies of sugar and coffee and candy were memories of the past, and their meager pay and inflation denied them an occasional, tension-relieving brawl. Their nagging, hard-working wives were driven to excessive carping by the sight of hungry children and gaunt husbands, whom they loved with women's selfless devotion. They would almost sell their souls for ham, bacon, meal, flour, and a few yards of cloth for a calico dress.

Although relatively few in number, the " poor white trash " of Richmond, the loafers and beggars, welcomed any opportunity to attain property without the debilitation of work. There were free Negroes, too, but most of them acted with circumspection in a white man's society. Desire for luxuries and need for provisions conquered restraint in a few of them. Thousands of slaves, better fed and housed than some of the poverty-stricken whites, possessed no stake in society. Their extra comforts depended upon handouts from the master class or came from petty larceny of their owners' stores. The slavery of their past had prepared them more for plunder than for good citizenship. And even some of the white elite, with houses in the aristocratic sections of Richmond, owned itchy fingers.

Patriotism, the institution of slavery, policemen, and the military had maintained order in overcrowded Richmond during the war. Patriotism was tired; slavery was already in its last agony; and the police disappeared on the morning of April 3, along with the fleeing Confederate soldiers. Now men and women made their own law as raw whiskey hit empty stomachs. Thousands of people lost their identities in the mob; they moved in an anonymous mass, following the loud-mouthed leader, swaying to the rhythm of anarchy, and plundering at will. Flames, heat, and smoke encouraged the raging crowd to spread the fire. Wind-borne flames jumped from house to house, leaping across streets; soon entire blocks were ablaze. The Nineteenth Virginia Militia, which was supposed to guard the city, disappeared. In the past four years there had been too many deaths; no soldier could now shoot his countryman. And only shooting could stop the frenzied mob. No law remained in Richmond.

Hungry people, frustrated by flames at the government warehouses, found other storehouses to plunder. They rushed into burning buildings, trampling each other like stampeding cattle, to grab whatever was near. They loaded themselves with loot, shoved their ways to air, or threw away what they had taken to snatch up more desirable commodities taken by others. Men, women, and children, white and black, carrying capacious bags, baskets, tubs, buckets, tin pans, and aprons, cursed and shoved each other. Men fought over the most desirable goods; crying, yelling, snarling, the mobs surged in and out of stores, ever moving and always destroying much that they saved from burning. The successful rolled away barrels of bacon, flour, molasses. Owners of carts and wheelbarrows loaded them with meal, coffee, and sugar. Occasionally a man still found a keg of whiskey.

Above the crowd the rearing flames cracked and hissed in a symphony of destruction. From the river front dense clouds of smoke rolled uphill, hiding the devouring flames. The flames leapt buildings and streets, as though possessed by demons determined to destroy all of Richmond. The arsenal with its several hundred carloads of shells lay in the path of the wind-borne fire. Around eight o'clock a terrific explosion was followed by the sound of bursting shells. Almost every minute one exploded, and it continued for hours; the reverberations reminded soldiers of a bombardment at the front. The mob hesitated in order to hear and to digest rumors—the Yankees were shelling the city, or the Confederates were shooting from across the river so as to leave nothing in Richmond for the Yankees.[2] But only for a moment did

[2] Time sequence is difficult to determine on the morning of April 3. Retreating Confederates, victorious Federals, and residents of Richmond did not record events at the time of their occurrence. According to some recollections the explosions of the ironclads and the powder magazine and the pillaging came shortly after midnight. After a study of many sources, the author believes the ironclads and powder magazine went up just before daylight. Their explosions brought out the crowd. The firing of warehouses and bridges and the pillaging took place after sunrise. These conclusions are based on articles in the Richmond *Evening Whig*; correspondents who talked with residents on April 3 and 4 and sent reports to the *New York Times, Herald,* and *Tribune*; Washington *Chronicle* and *Republican*; Baltimore *Clipper*; Philadelphia *Press* and *Inquirer*; Cincinnati *Gazette*; Chicago *Tribune,* and

it hesitate. The looters renewed their activity, spurred on by the repeated explosions. Bursting shells pushed bright fountains of light through the smoke, and the bursts were followed by deafening roars. Bits of shells sprayed the streets. Interspersed between explosions, cartridges rattled away, giving the impression of repeated volleys of musketry at the battlefront. The sides of two hills received most of the bullets and shells from the arsenal, situated as it was in a hollow, and the hills saved hundreds of pillagers from injury. But people were killed in Richmond. A shell fragment hit William Royster in the abdomen as he stood on his porch at the corner of Fourth and Carey streets. Judson Crane jumped to aid his fallen companion, and another fragment knocked him backward. A little Negro child stood alone, crying, in a vacant lot near Canal Street. She fell with bright red blood covering her faded dress and cried no more. In a four-hour bombardment more than 100,000 shells exploded, and shrapnel weighing several pounds dropped on Capitol Square. Miraculously only a few casualties resulted.

The intermittent noise of exploding shells and the crash of falling walls covered both the cries of hundreds of people who hurried to and fro with the pitiful relics of their household goods and the shouts of thousands bent only on plunder. The rioters cleaned out Confederate and private warehouses. The abundant rations, the bundles of blankets, clothing, and shoes hoarded by government and merchants, angered hungry, ragged people suffering from a scarcity of food and clothing. Why these bountiful warehouses when Lee's army fought barefooted and hungry? Why these luxuries hoarded

---

other Northern newspapers; J. B. Jones's *Diary*; the diaries of Emma Mordecai, Edward M. Boykin, Peter Helms Mayo, and others in the Southern Collection of the University of North Carolina; and a few reminiscences in the Virginia State Library and the Confederate Museum.

in stores when citizens were faint with hunger? These and other questions were not answered that day. The necessity of central storehouses and the inadequacy of Confederate transportation were not considered by the mob. The maddened people recalled the appeals of the past months, appeals endorsed by respected ministers of most churches, appeals to citizens to give corn, wheat, and meat that would feed soldiers at the front. Undoubtedly, the crowd thought, avaricious government agents had lived high on the hog while the people sacrificed. And officials were not the only guilty parties. What of the advertisements in newspapers of whiskey and brandy; what of stores filled with luxuries, of the wealthy dining on delicacies in hotel restaurants, of goods brought in by blockade-runners for private enjoyment? What of the storekeepers, those extortionists grown rich on the money of the needy? "The Jews," rang the cry, and those always-to-be-blamed scapegoats for the deficiencies of others were cursed again. There would be a grand redistribution of wealth this morning. The mob turned from empty warehouses to retail stores.

In an unreceding wave the mobsters moved. Deserters used gun butts to break in doors and shatter windows. One leader was a magnificently proportioned Negro who carried an iron bar on his shoulder and wore a bright red cloth around his waist, which hung down and flapped around his knees. The mob moved behind him as he advanced, and flowed through every door opened by his crowbar. In each store bolts of cloth, clothing, shoes, jewelry, furniture, tobacco, and other commodities were pulled from shelves and floors until the store was bare. The huge Negro took nothing himself but, king-like, watched his subjects and led them to new treasures. Maliciously, the mob's rear guard, angered by failure to obtain more, fired the ransacked stores.

Few looters saved as much as a tenth of their plunder. The gutters and sidewalks of Main Street were strewn with

Print by Confederate Museum

MR. AND MRS. JEFFERSON DAVIS
(This photograph was taken shortly after the war)

CITY HALL

Print by Valentine Museum

The spire in the background is on the Broad Street Methodist Church
at Tenth and Broad streets

VIEW OF THE CONFEDERATE WHITE HOUSE

Print by Valentine Museum

ST. PAUL'S EPISCOPAL CHURCH

ROCKETT'S AND THE JAMES RIVER

RICHMOND ON APRIL 2, 1865
The scene was taken from the south side of the James River

Joseph Mayo, Mayor of Richmond

Print by New York Public Library

ELIZABETH VAN LEW and the Garden of Her Mansion

THE BURNING OF RICHMOND

Print by Valentine Museum

PONTOON BRIDGE ACROSS THE JAMES RIVER

RICHMOND SKYLINE BY MATHEW BRADY
This view was taken from ruins of the Arsenal. The capitol is in the center of the picture and the spire of St. Paul's Church is on the left.

View in Richmond—From the Spottswood Hotel

The Ruins Along Main Street

silks, satins, bonnets, boots, hats, clothing, and groceries. Dirty feet ground fine cloth on the pavement, they bent and cracked jewelry, and kicked away hats and bonnets. Live coals fell on the cloth, and angry women ripped cotton goods in battles for possession. Men filled with liquor rolled casks and barrels or staggered under the burden of great loads of stolen goods. Boys and girls, half-stifled by smoke, tugged, pulled, and hauled at choice objects. They strained youthful backs trying to move heavy boxes of tobacco. Smoke-blackened women rolled barrels of flour, screeching to others for assistance, but seldom getting it unless a partnership in spoils was arranged. Carts, drays, and wheelbarrows raced in a continuous train out of the burning area. The greedy dropped their wares to grab more desirable stores that had been deposited on streets by those who rushed into stores for more. Thus, the plundered merchandise was stolen by other looters.

Owners who were threatened with the greatest loss seemed the least concerned as they saw their property scattered, divided among thieves, or trampled in the streets. They stood immobile in attitudes of unbelieving apathy. There were no guards, no policemen, nothing to stop the wholesale destruction. Rights in property had vanished. No one owned anything.

One proprietor leveled a shotgun at a soldier in the act of knocking in a window. But the deserter did not hesitate. With the crash of glass, a load of buckshot hit him in the belly. He clutched his stomach and fell with blood gushing through his fingers. No Samaritan stopped to aid a dying man. In a clothing store at the corner of Cary and Pearl streets a rioter fell through a hatchway and broke his neck. Black eyes, strained backs, sprained ankles, and bruised heads were numerous, but these came from brawls over plunder rather than from men defending their property.

In the tumult people apparently lost all reason. J. B.

Jones, the " Rebel War Clerk," was stopped by a woman on Broad Street. She offered him a bushel of potatoes for seventy-five dollars in Confederate currency. Although this price was five dollars less than that of Saturday, she insisted on the transaction; and Jones, who days before had snatched a half-eaten chicken from his cat, bought the potatoes. Aged Isaac Davenport refused to leave his room in the American Hotel. No one present could force the old man from the burning building. The crashing wall killed him instantly. Even some looters stopped to watch a gang of young men pulling coffins from an undertaker's establishment. But the energetic scoundrels filled the funeral boxes with a cache of stolen goods and dragged them away. A few drunks shed tears on seeing well-known saloons go up in flames. Tom Griffin's " Congress Hall," Charles Hunt's " Our House," Henry Smith's " The Place," and scores of others were devoured by the fire. No saloon of any reputation remained.

Like a whirlwind sweeping through the dead leaves of autumn, the hot wind scattered government records and letters in a paper tornado. Confederate bonds and paper money, bank notes and other currency littered the streets in every direction. They were so worthless that boys did not stoop to pick them up. Yet a few adults chased the tumbling bonds and notes and hid some of them in a furtive manner underneath their clothing.

And all the while the fire, fanned by the southeast breeze, swept from block to block. The red, round sun rose above the hills and hung like a beacon of woe, or like the awful accusing eye of an avenging God. Men stood, stunned and dumb, watching the rolling, surging sea of fire sweep away comforts accumulated by the toil of years. " Remorseless flame! What cared it for tears. It leaped for very joy; it leaped and danced upon the house tops; it shot up in great pyramids, and curled up and nestled down in chambers."

One observer viewing burning Richmond from a hill recalled old paintings depicting the terrors of Hell. The smoke of its torment hung in billowing clouds over acres of the city. " The Devil was loosed for his little season: God seemed to have removed his providence, and all was whirling to chaos and ruin together." Flames and smoke from the vehicular and railroad bridges drifted in almost parallel lines from the James River into distance.

A man standing near his house, the lower floor of which was his store, wept and wrung his hands. " Just look there! " he cried. " It's going to burn up my house and everything I've got in the world. I have worked hard twenty-five years and cheated nobody, and now I'm going to be robbed of all in a moment. Oh! God, it is too hard." As the flames enveloped the roof, he yelled in anguish and raised his arms. " There goes five hundred thousand dollars to Hell, and I haven't got one dollar in my pocket." His voice was partially stifled by smoke and tears as he turned to some young men. " Go in boys, go in. I'll give you a gold dollar for every piece of goods you save." The pillagers moved forward, but before they reached the building its crashing roof sent up a pillar of flame and smoke.

While the mob raged and plundered, homeowners in the path of the fire tried to save their household effects. Some of them deposited goods in the streets, and while they went back into the house for more, looters made away with the piles of clothing, cooking utensils, and furniture. Other more fortunate individuals carried their personal property to Capitol Square. There three hundred stricken families huddled in fear and fright around their meager belongings. Even on the emerald green lawn of early spring, the smoke and heat from the burning buildings on two sides of the square made the refugees most uncomfortable.

Rebecca Jane Allen with her four small children lived

at Twentieth and Main streets, only a block from Libby Prison. Her husband was fighting somewhere in the Confederate army. As the fire approached, she led her brood to a vacant lot across the street, seated them on some boards, and warned the youngsters not to catch cold by letting their feet touch the ground. They watched in awe as their mother made repeated trips to their house, disappearing inside and reappearing with armloads of goods. Then she hugged her young ones, as all of them watched the fire. The heat made the baby cry, but fortunately the flames spared the house; late in the afternoon the family returned to it.

Other houses apparently doomed were also saved. A teen-aged boy cleaned his mother's beds of blankets and spread them on the roof. He kept the blankets wet by pouring on buckets of water, and sparks hissed and went out upon touching the damp wool. Inside the house roomers hung dripping sheets over windows to shut out some of the smoke and cinders. This protection failed to keep out the smoke in another household, where an eighteen-year-old girl, recovering from typhoid fever, was carried into the street. She died before the end of the day. Admirers of General Lee formed a bucket brigade to water his house, while Mrs. Lee remained safely inside. Addison Hodge sat on the roof of his uncle's house at Fifth and Main with a bucket of water and tin cup to douse any spark he saw.

From the rooftop Addison could almost touch Moses Hodge's Second Presbyterian Church. Three blocks north he saw the spire of the United Presbyterian Church. Only the afternoon before, he recalled, the Presbyterians of Richmond had met at the United for prayer. Now he watched the flames dancing up the shingled steeple. It swayed and tottered as if undecided whether to fall into the street or backward upon the main roof. Backward it went, and the church was soon a smoking ruin.

Across the street Mrs. Robert Stanard sat on a trunk. As the flames had come near her house, she had packed in the trunk her most precious jewels and her best dresses. A servant had carried the trunk to the pavement, and Mrs. Stanard left her costly and tastefully furnished home. Now the former Martha Pierce of Kentucky recalled past evenings of triumph, as she watched the burning church. Vice-President Alexander H. Stephens, Judah P. Benjamin, L. Q. C. Lamar, various senators and representatives, statesmen and military officers, and many distinguished foreign visitors had fallen under her magnetic spell. A friend offered her assistance, but she assured him that she was unafraid. Attired in a stunning dress, a fashionable bonnet, a thin veil, and long gloves, she peered through her lorgnette at the progressing conflagration, which would mark the end of an era in Richmond. The young, beautiful, and propertied widow would soon shift the locale of her parties from the doomed capital of the Confederacy to the booming one of the United States.

She was more fortunate than many Richmonders who possessed little money other than Confederate currency. In past weeks some far-sighted people had exchanged their notes for gold at the rate of sixty-five dollars in currency for one of gold. By this Monday morning even illiterate Negroes were refusing Confederate bills. Major John King was entrusted with some Treasury Department archives. In vain he searched for a government wagon as the fire neared his house. Finally he met " Jehu " mounted on a dilapidated cart and apparently awaiting customers.

" Come on, boy! " King shouted. " I'll give you fifty dollars."

Jehu saw the Confederate notes and replied: " Why dat won't pass, Massa. What use is dat to me? "

" Well then, Buck, here's a hundred; that's worth something. Come on. Don't you see my place is burning down? "

" Have to let it burn, Massa, but I can't take a hundred."

" Here take three hundred, five hundred, a thousand dollars."

But the Negro did not move until the Major pulled a pistol on him. Then slowly Jehu pulled his cart along, following King, pleading with him. " Haven't you got any old clothes you'd give me instead of dat Confederate trash? Any little trick you have about you in the shape of a watch-guard or a ring, or something to eat."

Major King never saved the treasury papers, but he did flee from the city. Walking west, he passed many disheartened men sitting on baggage beside broken wagons or carts. That way, too, lay many wrecked commissary transports. Edward Hitchcock McDonald passed one filled with shoes. He and his companion loaded their buggy with them. Later he discovered that three pairs of boots would buy a quick repair of a crushed wheel by a blacksmith who left other jobs to earn the shoes. The smith preferred them to $2,500 in Confederate currency.

But not everyone was running *from* Richmond. After a night of fear at their plantation Emma Mordecai and her sister-in-law Rosina decided that Augusta should be sent to relatives inside the city. A young girl, they reasoned, would be more protected from " barbaric " Yankee soldiers in Richmond than on a farm. Rosina owned a barrel of flour at Mr. Gordon's store in town and a box of valuable plate in one of the city banks. She was anxious to secure them before the " vandals " overran Richmond. The women packed a trunk and a carpetbag for Augusta and penned orders on Mr. Gordon and the bank. Emma and Augusta left in a covered cart drawn by a lazy mule and driven by George, a slave of the plantation. They met soldiers walking, generally in pairs, loaded with assorted possessions. " You're going to a bad place," the soldiers warned. " The Yankees are expected soon."

Emma sighted the clouds of smoke ascending over Richmond. She knew that stores of tobacco and cotton were to be burned, but she could not understand the cause of the bursting shells. At Camp Lee the white tents of yesterday, occupied by exchange Confederate prisoners of war, were now deserted. Further on, two women told Emma that they were leaving the city, for it was no place for unprotected ladies with all the Yankee soldiers coming. A slave would not be bothered, they stated, but Emma and Augusta would be wise to return to their home. George's eyes had lit up on hearing about the looting; no entreaties or commands could make him turn back. Augusta's baggage was stored with a family named Luck, new and unknown residents in the area, who promised to care for it. Emma told George to go on with the cart, do the errands, and if possible get some bacon and flour from the commissary warehouses. Emma and Augusta turned back toward home.

Down the road they met a young Negro woman, who asked: " Mam, you gwine away from dem nasty-Yankees? "

" We are going home," Emma replied. " Where are you going? "

" I'm gwine to town to hunt my young mistress. I'd risk my life to git her from dem terrible Yankees."

Augusta burst into tears and sobbed her way home. The women packed their valuables in two trunks, but there was no good place of concealment, so they left the keys in the locks to prevent marauding Federal soldiers from breaking them open.

Unnoticed during the excitement in and out of Richmond, Mayor Mayo buttoned the brass buttons of his blue coat, put on a large white hat, and joined some other men in a surrey. They skirted the fire on Main Street and drove to the Osborne Road. With a small piece of white cloth flying on a stick, they moved down the road in search of some Union officers to whom they could surrender the city.

CAPTURE

MAJOR GENERAL GODFREY WEITZEL commanded the Federal troops on the north side of the James River only a few miles from Richmond. A native of Cincinnati, Ohio, the twenty-nine-year-old general was a graduate of West Point. Before the war he had served under P. G. T. Beauregard, constructing forts Jackson and St. Phillip on the Mississippi below New Orleans. He participated in the bombardment of Fort Sumter in 1864, and aided Butler near Wilmington, North Carolina, in attacking Fort Fisher. His ability won him command of the Army of the James, many of whose troops were former slaves.

The thought of ex-slaves in Federal uniform marching on the capital of the South pleased the editor of the Cincinnati *Daily Gazette*. The Confederacy, he wrote, was founded upon slavery, and Richmond was the center of the slave-aristocracy. Imagine the scene, the editor continued: the slave drivers with their garments gathered up about them moving double quick out of one side of the city as their former slaves, with heads erect, guns in hand, and powder dry, marched in the other side under the national banner and to the music of the Union. It was a picture of humiliation and retribution on one hand, he concluded, and of triumph and victory on the other, which " will receive a special page in history."

Weitzel was more immediately concerned with the capture of Richmond than with his place in history. The musical concert of Confederate bands on Sunday night had puzzled him. He knew of General Lee's precarious situation at Petersburg, but he did not dream that the long-sought victory was so near. Communications from his commander, General Grant, were always slow in arriving. At three o'clock in the morning of April 3 a Confederate deserter claimed that Lee was withdrawing from Petersburg under cover of darkness. Weitzel realized that this retreat, if actual, foreshadowed the evacuation of Richmond, but one could not rely on the tale of a deserter. An hour later, however, the Confederate tents in front of his position went up in flames, and then scouts rode in with authentic reports of hasty and general retreat from the southern breastwork defenses of the city.

The moon had set three hours earlier. Weitzel, a general who really cared for the safety of his men, feared numerous casualties from Confederate mines in the darkness. He ordered early breakfasting and immediate preparation for marching. For months he had waited for this day. His patience could continue now until daylight, to save the lives of his soldiers. Near dawn the terrific explosions in Richmond emphasized the fact that the city was being evacuated.

As dawn lit the sky he sent out skirmishers to feel their way through Confederate fortification. The General's precaution in not advancing until daylight proved to be a wise decision. Enemy mines covered the ground so completely that the soldiers moved in single file. The infernal devices were marked for them by sticks with pieces of red webbing attached. These markers placed for the protection of Confederate soldiers were forgotten in the fast retreat.

The Federals found seven distinct lines of earthen fortifications that had protected Richmond. Nearly all were covered with last summer's decaying vegetation, and some were gullied by heavy spring rains. The three outer lines almost circled Richmond; the four inner ones consisted of redoubts and bastion forts. Many guns remained in position, and the skirmishers found guns, pistols, letters, and diaries of the retreating foe. Several of the front lines were protected by barricades which were made by driving sharply hewn stakes, about eight feet long, through a long log in such a way that six of them projected from a common center like spokes from a hub. The logs, laid end to end, formed one long hub extending for miles, each log resting on its sharpened spokes. The staves radiated so thickly that unless they had been broken by artillery fire, a soldier could barely creep through them. If he rolled them over, he only turned up other spokes to meet him in the face.

After the skirmishers had made paths through these obstructions and had cleared avenues through the mine fields, Weitzel ordered the advance. Brigades of the Twenty-fourth and Twenty-fifth corps advanced over the Confederate works and took positions on the Osborne Road, New Market Road, and Darkytown Pike. General Weitzel sent Majors A. H. Stevens and E. E. Graves with forty cavalrymen to scout these roads, all of which led to Richmond. At the junction of the New Market and Osborne roads, just behind the former Confederate lines, the Federals saw a shabby carriage approaching with its driver waving a white flag of truce. The time was eight-fifteen. In the vehicle were Mayor Mayo, Judge John A. Meredith of the Superior Court in Richmond, James Lyons, and a few other Richmond dignitaries. They announced themselves ready to surrender the city to Federal authority.

"Who is in command of this flag of truce?" Major Stevens demanded.

"Mr. Mayo, Mayor of the city of Richmond," Judge Meredith replied.

He introduced the mayor and his associates to Stevens and Graves. Mayo extended a paper to Stevens who accepted it and read: "Richmond. Monday, April 3, 1865. To the General Commanding the United States Army in front of Richmond: General, The Army of the Confederate Government having abandoned the City of Richmond, I respectfully request that you will take possession of it with an organized force, to preserve order and protect women and children and property. Respectfully, Joseph Mayo, Mayor."

Major Stevens stated that the document was acceptable and promised it would be delivered to General Weitzel. The mayor and his party turned back toward Richmond. At ten o'clock he would repeat the surrender to General Weitzel himself on the portico of the Virginia capitol.

On receiving the Major's report, Weitzel ordered a general advance, and divisions raced to be the first to enter Richmond. Other than a few stray and harmless shots by stragglers, the Federals met no opposition. Most of the stragglers appeared happy to surrender as the Twenty-fourth and Twenty-fifth corps pressed forward. Brevet Brigadier General A. G. Draper's colored infantry of the Twenty-fifth Corps took the lead, but the white troops determined to have the glory of initial entry. Their officers obtained an order for Draper to move his troops to the left side of the road to make room for the First Brigade, Third Division, Twenty-fourth Corps, of General Edward Hastings Ripley. Draper obeyed, but moved his brigade in double time, knowing it would not be overtaken. Before Ripley's command caught them, the Negro troops entered the outskirts of Richmond, stacked their arms, and watched the white soldiers pass. The Third Division continued to the heart of the city, led by a band playing patriotic airs.

Major Stevens' cavalry rode ahead up Main Street. The Major stopped to inquire the way to the capitol, wheeled his command up Governor Street and then into Capitol Square. For lack of a flag he hoisted two guidons over the statehouse. Later General George Foster Shepley raised the first flag over the capitol. It was the same standard which he had wagered at the beginning of the war he would plant over the St. Charles Hotel in Charleston. Later he had bet it would also float over Richmond. He won both bets.

In time others claimed the honor of hoisting the first United States flag over captured Richmond. Richard G. Forrester, a Negro page of the Virginia legislature, told a Federal lieutenant that he had kept the old flag, lowered on the secession of Virginia, hidden in his bed for almost four years. After the Confederates withdrew on April 3, he ran from his house at Marshall and College streets, climbed the capitol stairs, and attached the flag to the tall staff on the roof. Elizabeth Van Lew claimed that she had ordered and secreted a twenty-five-foot flag. An hour before the first Union troops entered the city, she ran it up on the east side, near Rockett's, so that the soldiers marching up Main Street could greet it. No Federal officer mentioned either of these flags in his report.

The people of Richmond received General Weitzel with various emotions. Thousands of Negroes danced with joy on seeing their brothers-in-arms. Bands playing " Yankee Doodle," " John Brown's Body," or the " Battle Hymn of the Republic," were greeted with ear-shattering cheers. " Such cheers rent the air as they passed along as can only be given by the oppressed when relieved of their cruel oppressors," one Northerner reported. Men waved their hats and women their hands in tokens of their happiness. Pious Negroes of both sexes shouted: " You've come at last, Glory, Hallelujah! " " Jesus has opened the way! " " We've been looking for you these many days! " " Thank God! " " I've not seen the old flag in four years, it does my eyes good! "— and similar expressions.

Looking from her window, a young white woman shuddered in disgust to see Negroes falling before the " invaders," hailing them as deliverers, embracing the knees of horses, and almost keeping the troops from moving forward. " Was it to this end," she asked, " we had fought and starved and gone naked and cold? To this end that the wives and children of many dear and gallant friends were husbandless and fatherless? To this end that our homes were in ruins, our state devastated? "

On seeing the first Yankee ride by dressed in his blue jacket with yellow stripes down the back, Emmie Crump ran into her house and slammed all the shutters. She and her mother considered themselves in a state of siege. They alternated the voicing of their fears with peeking through the shutters at the regiments marching up Governor and Broad streets. Their free Negro servant told Emmie's mother: "Don't be scared. I done told de soldiers you is a good Union woman." This form of assurance so angered the women that they wanted to hang out a Confederate flag. But they held back for fear of retribution.

White people in the Rockett's area cheered the Federal troops as they entered the eastern and poorer part of the city. Most frequently, however, a cry of distress—"The Yankees! Oh! the Yankees have come! "—preceded the troops. As the soldiers passed on and took control of Richmond, some of the more watchful ones saw many persons in finer houses peeping out of windows. One observer thought the movements of these defeated people should be watched, for there " was no mistaking the curl of their lips and the flash of their eyes." A few " loud-mouthed and hasty rebs " got themselves in trouble by too free a use of their tongues and were confined by the provost marshal. Richmond people gaped in wonder at the splendidly equipped army marching under the old flag. At first sight of the flag and first sound of the old familiar tunes, patriotism reawakened in many breasts, but on second thought came the " dreadful realization " that the " Star Spangled Banner " was a requiem for buried Southern hopes.

Occupation of Richmond did not meet the expectations of many Northern soldiers. Entering the city near the height of the fire, cavalrymen protected their faces from the intense heat which seemed to be searing their hair and mustaches. The shacks in Rockett's, dirty people, and paper-littered streets made a poor prize for all the years of fighting. Roaring flames, dense smoke, and exploding shells seemed to cheat the victors in their hour of triumph. Yet the roaring and dashing and clashing, the burning and trembling buildings, the shouts of comrades marching up Main Street, the stirring martial music of the bands, the shouts of welcome—all the bustle of occupying the enemy capital city etched themselves deeply into memories of Northern soldiers. The taking of Richmond, the object of four years of struggle in hard-fought battles at the cost of many thousands of lives, sent quivers racing up and down Yankee spines. On reaching Capitol Square, officers rushed to embrace each other, slapped backs in expressions of delight, and exchanged congratulations on the peaceful occupation. Tears of joy ran down the cheeks of some of the older soldiers. Enlisted men cheered lustily, capered in delight, or amused themselves by asking where Jeff Davis was.

General Weitzel stood on the high steps at the east side of the state capitol and looked down into the crater of fire. The volume of smoke and cinders made breathing difficult and impaired the vision. After establishing his headquarters in the hall of the House of Delegates, he issued orders for the pacification and control of the city. His first order stated:

Major General Godfrey Weitzel, commanding detachment of the Army of the James, announces the occupation of the city of Richmond by the armies of the United States under command of Lieutenant General Grant. The people of Richmond are assured that we come under the flag of the Union. The citizens of Richmond are requested to remain for the present quietly within their houses, and to avoid all public assemblages or meetings in the public streets. An efficient provost guard will immediately establish order and tranquility within the city. Martial law is for the present proclaimed. Brigadier General George F. Shepley, U. S. Volunteers, is hereby appointed military governor of Richmond. Lt. Col. Frederick S. Manning, Provost Marshal General of the Army of the James will act as Provost Marshal of Richmond. Commanders of detachments doing guard duty in the city will report to him for instructions.

The immediate concerns of Military Governor Shepley were the fire and the riot. General Ripley with his brigade of 300 officers and 4,200 men, were assigned the task of restoring order in Richmond. Ripley asked General Weitzel to station all other troops in the inner defense works just outside the city and to forbid the re-entry of soldiers. Taking Mayor Mayo with him, Ripley established his headquarters in the city hall. He stationed his regiments at key points within the city with orders to warn everyone to go to their houses and to arrest whenever necessary those who would not. He sent staff officers to inspect the fire department. To Ripley his job seemed almost impossible with the headway already made by the fire and with the powder and shells stored within the burning city. The explosions continued "like a contest of innumerable artillery, like that which preceded Pickett's memorable assault at Gettysburg, and was awe-inspiring, punctuated by the heavier explosions of the ironclads in the river."

In his first order of the day General Shepley stated that the armies of the rebellion had abandoned their efforts to enslave the people of Virginia and had attempted to destroy the capital of the state. He called on the fire department and all citizens interested in saving their beautiful city to report for duty and render every possible assistance. The first duty of the Union army, he promised, would be to save the city doomed to destruction by the army of the rebellion.

To Provost Marshal Manning fell the primary responsibility of checking the flames. On orders from Manning, Major Stevens sounded the alarm bell. Only a few firemen responded. The fire-fighting equipment consisted of two steam engines, four useless hand engines, and quantities of ruined hose. Without pumping engines or hose, the fire could not be put out; it could only be contained and allowed to burn itself out. A study of the existing fires, the wind, streets, and vacant lots determined the action. Bucket brigades threw water on unfired buildings rather than on the burning ones. Whenever the heat permitted close work, wooden walls were battered down to keep the flames low. And a few untouched buildings were leveled by explosives. At certain points, back fires were set to the debris. Even the most anti-Unionist Richmonder admitted that the Federal soldiers labored hard and bravely. Within four hours an almost cleared path surrounded the burning areas. Unless the wind increased tremendously, the fire could do no more than burn and smolder in the already destroyed sections of Richmond. Fortunately the breeze subsided, and the fire was contained.

An efficient military police force also helped to save Richmond. Too much blame for the fire may have been laid to the wind and too little to pillagers. Between Twentieth and Twenty-second streets, where plundering was minor, only a block and a half burned. In the more devastated areas the plunderers undoubtedly fired many buildings. Shepley's soldier-policemen scoured the city, ordering people to go home, arresting Confederate stragglers, and recapturing escaped convicts. By nightfall more than a hundred of the latter, and thousands of straggler-deserters, who had been the core of the mob, crowded Libby Prison and Castle Thunder. All persons arrested with stolen property were taken to city hall, where the goods were described and stored. By proclamation it was announced that any citizen or Confederate soldier who continued to plunder, destroy, or remove any public or private property would be arrested and summarily punished. The speed and efficiency of the Federal soldiers, together with their discipline, soon cleared the streets of loiterers and rioters.

The guards neither tried nor could recapture all stolen property. As they worked to restore order, whites and Negroes carried away their loot and secreted it in their houses. Many Richmond families ate well on Monday. Some people got enough to clothe and feed themselves for months. Others sold their plunder for greenbacks to newly arrived Northern sutlers. But hundreds of unfortunate victims congregated in Capitol Square, homeless, propertyless, and foodless. The riot did not produce wealth. It destroyed, and for every one who gained, ten suffered.

The high command of the Army of the James occupied the better houses in Richmond. Weitzel, his aides, and Military Governor Shepley took over the abandoned Confederate White House. They appreciated the cleanliness and excellent condition of the house and examined with interest the ornaments which Mrs. Davis had used to decorate mantles and tables. Many of these ornaments disappeared to reappear as mementos in the homes of Northern officers. General Charles Devens moved into the governor's mansion, but he did not evict Mrs. Smith and her daughter. They moved voluntarily because the house belonged to the state. Provost Marshal Manning established his headquarters in the Hall of Delegates in the capitol building, and Ripley remained in the city hall. Other officers rented quarters in private houses.

One Richmond girl later gave her recollections of a drunken Federal soldier who claimed that he and his companions were searching for Confederate deserters. After entering her house, he touched the girl's arm and whispered: " Sis, I'm good Secesh as you but don't say nothin' about it."

" You better look thoroughly," the girl replied, pretending not to hear, and throwing up the mattress on a bed so that he could see no one was hidden underneath.

" Good Secesh as you is Sis. I ain't agwine to look into nothin', Sis."

" There's nothing for you to find," the girl declared. She led him to another room where a boy was cleaning a gun.

" Better hide that, Sonny," the inebriated soldier warned. " That other fellow out there, he'll take it from you. I won't take nothin'. I'm good Secesh as you is, bud. Hide your gun."

The soldier left to search the rooms of a Mrs. Sampson, who gave him a tongue-lashing for overturning furniture. The angry woman reported the incident to General Weitzel, who assured her that the man must be a Union straggler. If found, Weitzel promised, he would be punished for searching the house without authority.

General Shepley prohibited the use of offensive words or insulting gestures by his men. No home could be searched without an order from him or from the provost marshal. And citizens were ordered on pain of swift punishment to utter no treasonable or offensive expressions, insulting to the United States flag, the cause, or the Federal soldiers. Civilians must secure passes to enter or leave the city. Even Union soldiers tented in the outskirts needed permission to visit Richmond.

By midafternoon order returned to the Virginia capital. Only a few incidents marred relations between conqueror and conquered. Many Confederate officers gained freedom of the city by giving their paroles of honor. Some Southern naval officers were arrested at the Spottswood Hotel while attempting to drown their sorrows. They vociferously objected to walking under guard through the streets and demanded transportation in a carriage. Yet after a warning by the provost marshal they were paroled. Some officers of high rank, former guards of Federal prisoners of war, and officers refusing to sign paroles were confined to Libby Prison.

As overall commander, Weitzel extended his lines beyond Richmond. A brigade of colored troops took positions across the James. The truce steamer *William Allison*, the only remaining ship at the navy yard, carried a detachment of cavalry to Manchester where it seized thirty abandoned cannon. Rear Admiral David Dixon Porter co-operated with the army by removing obstructions and torpedoes in the James. By nightfall the river was clear to within a few miles of Richmond.

Hours before dark the orderliness of Richmond permitted some relaxation of regulations. Citizens could move through the streets if there was a good reason. Ladies who imagined a barbaric horde of Union soldiers bent on acts of medieval rapine implored protection from Shepley or Manning. Their pleas received polite attention, and soldiers were assigned to escort them to their homes. Negro or white guards posted at the center of every block were responsible for the safety of each neighborhood. Many of the sentinels discovered destitute families and shared their rations with them. Although the guards were not specially selected men, Shepley asserted later that he never received a single complaint of rudeness or misbehavior on their part. Without a request, guards were posted at the home of Mrs. Lee.

Another woman knew that *she* needed no protection. Threats of Confederate sympathizers to burn Miss Van Lew's house were stilled, and neighbors came to borrow her wheelbarrow and cart. They returned with loads of valuables and pleas for " Crazy Bet " to hide their property from the Yankee vandals. Failing to convince her neighbors of Northern honesty, she granted their wishes. Undoubtedly officers and men visited her during the day to thank her for past Union activities. Anyone else would have rested that day, but she walked uptown to search for Confederate archives, to gather un-issued bonds, and for personal satisfaction to sketch a pro-posed Confederate flag. She viewed the devastation left by the fire and saw the cloud of smoke as incense rising from the city in thanksgiving for its deliverance. In the evening she wrote:

What a moment! Avenging wrath appeared in flames. The chains, the shackles fell from thousands of captives—minds and bodies both freed—and thousands of arms fell powerless to wield the *Christianizing* lash. Civilization advanced a century—justice, truth, humanity was vindicated. Labor was now without mana-cles, honored and respected. No wonder the walls of our house were swaying; the heart of our city a flaming altar, as His mighty work was done. Oh! Army of my country, how glorious was your welcome. The wonderful deliverance wrought for the Negro[es], they feel but cannot tell you, but when eternity shall unroll the record of time you will see written for them by the Almighty their unpenned stories, then to be read before a listening uni-verse. Bottled are their tears; on His ear fell their groans, though the earth scarcely received their echo.

Crazy Bet sang her joy alone in Richmond. Other citi-zens heeded the nine o'clock curfew. Some counted their gains of the morning in food and clothing. Others wondered where provisions could be secured on the morrow. Women still fearful thanked God for deliverance from insult and outrage during the past hours, but dreaded what their imagi-nations envisioned for the future. Guards walked their rounds on quiet, lonely streets. Fires smouldered from Main Street to the river. The moon dipped lower and lower against the dark sky as stars brightened over the occupied city of Richmond.

WASHINGTON

A HUNDRED MILES north of Richmond, in the capital above the Potomac, the morning calm of April 3 foretold no midafternoon madness. Readers of the *Morning Chronicle* scanned headlines for war news as they had daily during the war. They lingered on details of Grant's victories near Petersburg and President Lincoln's letter from City Point. The *Chronicle*'s editorials were optimistic, and Washingtonians of 1865 read editorials.

Under the heading " The Policy of Mercy " the editor told his patrons that history proved mercy and clemency to a foe were of value. With or without further efforts toward reconciliation, he stated, " it is most desirable that the tone of the press, the pulpit, and the rostrum should show that the Northern people are capable of a magnanimity worthy of a great and free nation . . . a magnanimity that shall carry with it the conclusive proof that we have not degenerated [during the war] to the frantic barbarity of a state of anarchy, or to the cruelty inseparable from despotism." In another editorial, " The Last Ditch," the *Chronicle* reviewed the recent victories of Grant and Sheridan. " Lee is defeated," the editor proclaimed, for

the last ditch has finally been reached. The wretched and misguided men who have for four years devoted themselves to the cause of rebellion may continue for an indefinite period to accept the last ditch as their final resting place, and by a system of guerrilla warfare and brigandage, lead an infamous life and gain a precarious subsistence. But the days are passed when public opinion praised the obstinacy of the Highlanders and called it heroism. The rebels have been firmly beaten in a fair fight. It may be weeks or months before the contest is finally concluded, and we do not pretend that we are out of the woods yet; but one thing is clear, that the peace the rebels have so long been desiring is now within their reach; they can have it as soon as they ask it. A childish obstinacy may prolong their agonies, but their final success is now out of the question.

Many readers dismissed the editorial as another of those often-repeated promises of victory. More real to them were the *Chronicle*'s advertisements. Horace Greeley's first volume of *The American Conflict: A History of the Great American Rebellion* was on sale at Morrison's Bookstore. Grover's new theater announced that Effie German, after weeks of rehearsal, would star that evening in *Aladdin, or The Wonderful Lamp* in a " style of unsurpassed magnificence." At Ford's Theater the popular Laura would take the lead in *The Workmen of Washington,* an adaptation of the famous *Workmen of Paris.* For family entertainment Stone and Rosston's circus and Thayer, Noyes, and Van Amburg's circus and menagerie were performing at Sixth Street near New York Avenue. The gay crowd could dance or listen to the singing of " O'Flannigan at the Fair, or the Peep O'Day Boys " at Canterbury Hall. The Oxford Music Hall offered slack-wire and gymnastic performances in addition to singing and dancing.

For most Washingtonians these attractions, or a quiet evening at home, were still twelve hours away. Government clerks, businessmen, laborers, and school children trooped to their various activities and wholeheartedly agreed with the *Chronicle* that the dusty streets of the city were a constant affliction to pedestrians. In no part of Washington was the dust so thick as on Pennsylvania Avenue. Certainly, the *Chronicle* concluded, this business and promenade artery should be sprinkled frequently by water wagons.

Young William E. Kettles of Burlington, Vermont, shook grit from his coat before entering the telegraph office in the War Department. Kettles claimed the age of fourteen, but fellow workers thought that he stretched his years by one or two. Yet he was a full-fledged telegrapher. On the morning of April 3 his keys tapped out a message from President Lincoln: " This morning General Grant reports Petersburg evacuated, and he is confident Richmond is also. He is pushing forward to cut off the retreating army." Secretary of War Stanton received the message and forwarded its contents to Major General J. A. Dix in New York. At ten-forty-five young Kettles ran to the Secretary with General Weitzel's announcement of the capture of Richmond. After so many years of hope the news brought cheers from the War Department staff. Yet some doubted its authenticity; perhaps Confederate operators were sending a false report on Federal wires. Confirmation of the evacuation was requested from City Point. At eleven the reply came: " General Weitzel telegraphs as follows: ' We took Richmond this morning; I captured many guns. The enemy left in great haste. The city is on fire in one place—am making every effort to put it out. The people received us with enthusiastic expressions of joy.' "

From this moment Washington celebrated. Stanton gave the War Department clerks the rest of the day off. Secretary of the Interior John P. Usher said he could not expect anyone to work after hearing such news. Clerks in the departments paid their respects to secretaries and heads of bureaus, cheered and shouted until the corridors rang, sang " John Brown's Body " and " The Year of Jubilee," and then flowed out into the streets to tell the people the reason for their exuberance. On learning the good news, firemen rang the bell of the Metropolitan hook-and-ladder house on Massachusetts Avenue. New steam engines from this and other fire stations paraded the principal streets, and blew their whistles in triumph.

Impromptu processions formed and marched along the avenues. Men sang or shouted their joy; bells rang in church steeples and firehouses; engines whistled and cannon boomed. There was no concert anywhere, but every demonstration was spontaneous. From Camp Barry came a three-hundred-gun salute for the capture of Petersburg followed by one of five hundred guns for the capture of Richmond. The battery at the Navy Yard wharf fired a hundred-gun salvo. Superior Court Judge David Kellogg Cartter adjourned his court for the afternoon, as did the judge of the criminal court. School-teachers dismissed their classes on getting news of the victory, but one woman teacher refused to grant her pupils a holiday. Those who heard about it muttered against her and suggested an investigation of her loyalty. The veteran reserve corps marched in full-dress parade with happy mien and vigorous step. Army bands moved from corner to corner to play patriotic airs. Foreign ministers called on the Secretary of State to offer congratulations.

Some dubious citizens questioned the victory until they saw the four o'clock extra of the *Chronicle* with its headlines: " Glorious Fall of Richmond—Captured by Black Troops." Then the city seemed to explode. All classes, ages, sexes, and colors vied with each other in enthusiastic demonstrations. Negroes went wild and greeted with shouts and expressions of pride the entry of their brethren into the " citadel of their former slave masters." In a voice choked with emotion an old woman said: " God bless Massa Abraham and General Grant; they can't whip me any more, on the order of my old Massa in Richmond." Another Negro danced to his repeated cry of " De day of jubelo am come."

Flags were flying on every public building and on many private dwellings and places of business. During the remaining hours of daylight the crowd, carrying flags and banners, paraded in the streets. In a mass the milling, celebrating throng moved from building to building and from house to house. Bands played and *a cappella* choirs sang patriotic tunes and war songs. Handsomely outfitted horsemen from the Eastern Branch Corral honored the *Chronicle* with three cheers and then rode off in a cloud of dust to salute other establishments.

As was customary in an age of speechmaking, the people called on prominent officials to say something. At the War Department building a Negro girl amused onlookers by dancing to the rhythm of her clapping hands and shouting: " Bress God, the nigger's free. No more hoeing of corn for dis pore child, and no more lashes from dat cruel overseer." Former Senator Preston King of New York told the cheering people, " It was a fit consummation that both at Richmond and Charleston, the rebels surrendered to Negro troops. . . ." Senator James Warren Nye of Nevada said it was impossible to find expression for the feelings in his heart, but politician that he was, he spoke at length. Four years ago, he cried, " I stood alone to defend the capital and the Nation from a rebellious and bitter enemy. . . . The north then had no money or army; but, as if by magic, both had sprung up, and were of such magnitude as to astound the world, and the rebellion had at last succumbed to the liberty-loving people of the Union. Instead of witnessing in Richmond today the stars and bars floating from the public buildings, the stars and stripes are proudly waving in the breeze, and will there remain hereafter. It was written by the finger of God. In the midst of confusion and bloodshed He had exclaimed, ' It is I: be not afraid.' . . . Richmond today was held by Negro troops," the Senator concluded, " and it was fit for a city filled with traitors to their country."

The band of the Ninth Reserve Corps formed at the north corner of the War Department building and serenaded Secretary Stanton with stirring, patriotic music. The crowd yelled for the Secretary. The usually cold, calculating, but efficient Stanton appeared and spoke in a voice filled with emotion. In this hour of triumph, he said, the people should thank God, President Lincoln, and the gallant officers and men for victory. " Henceforth our commiseration and our aid should be given to the wounded, the maimed, and the suffering, who bear the marks of their great sacrifices in this mighty struggle. Let us humbly offer up thanks to Divine Providence, for his care over us, and beseech Him that He will guide and govern us . . . that He will teach us how to be humble in the midst of triumph, how to be just in the hour of victory. . . . Let us not forget the laboring millions in other lands, who, in this struggle, have given us their sympathies, their aid, and their prayers. . . ."

Stanton then read a telegram from General Grant announcing the capture of Richmond at eight-fifteen and the fire burning in that city.

" What answer shall I return to General Grant? " he asked.

" Let it burn! " was the impulsive response. But as an afterthought, here and there was a cry of " No, no don't destroy it! We can make good use of it! "

Stanton introduced telegraph operator Willie Kettles. " Have him speak! Let us hear him! " the crowd shouted. Willie declined. " He couldn't speak; he felt so." He acknowledged repeated cheers with a grateful bow, and a reporter saw in his expression a hearty love of country and an appreciation of the position he occupied.

Satisfied by these appearances the throng moved to the National Hotel. There a number of politicians regaled them with oratory. " This was a glorious day," Judge John Fitch Kinney of Utah exclaimed, " rendered doubly glorious by the fact, that with the fall of Richmond, falls the rebellion. It was a glorious day when the gallant navy took New Orleans

. . . a glorious day when the indomitable Sherman took Savannah . . . a glorious day when the city of Charleston, the ' Nestor ' city of the rebel States, yielded . . . a glorious day when Sherman with his unconquerable army marched trippingly into Columbia, but far more glorious . . . [is] this 3rd day of April, 1865 [when] the rebel capital, the ' Sebastopol ' of the South, was captured. . . . While the 4th day of July has been celebrated as the day that gave birth to a nation's freedom, we have this day added another, which, through all time, will mark another epoch in the history of great events . . . the 3rd of April, a day ever memorable in history as one which, by the skill of our generals and the courage of our soldiers preserved us a nation by giving the rebellion its mortal blow."

The people moved on to William H. Seward at the State Department. " I am now writing my foreign dispatches," he told them. " What shall I say to the Emperor of the French? "

" To get out of Mexico! " a voice replied.

" I shall say to the Emperor of the French, that he can go tomorrow to Richmond and get his tobacco, so long held under the blockade there, provided the rebels have not used it up." Laughter and cheers spurred the Secretary. " To Lord John Russell I will say that British Merchants will find the cotton exported from our ports under treaty with the United States cheaper than cotton obtained by running the blockade. . . . I need not tell him that this is a war for freedom and national independence and the right of nations, and not a war for empire; and if Great Britain should only be just to the United States, Canada will remain undisturbed by us so long as she prefers the authority of the noble Queen to voluntary incorporation into the United States."

" That's the talk! " the crowd shouted. " You're right! "

" I do not doubt, my fellow citizens," Seward continued,

" but that at last you accede to the theory by which I have governed myself during the war, namely that the rebellion will end in ninety days." Finally Seward told his laughing audience, " I will say that our motto in peace shall be what our text has been while in war. Every nation is entitled to regulate its own domestic affairs in its own way, and all are bound to conduct themselves so as to promote peace on earth and good will to mankind."

The crowd cheered, fell in behind a flag-bearer, and proceeded to the Willard Hotel. The cry went up for General Benjamin F. Butler, who appeared to harangue his eager listeners. Those who brought the great expenditure of blood and treasure upon the country, he said, should never be accorded political power to " again tear down the flag that waves over us. God rules by means, and a more striking rule of justice we have not seen than that Weitzel's corps of negro soldiers were the first to enter Richmond."

Vice-President Andrew Johnson was discovered in the crowd. Tired, somewhat embittered, Johnson recalled the poverty of his youth, the condescending attitude of wealthy planters, and his love of the Union. He mounted a portico and spoke with vindictiveness.

You must indulge me in making one single remark in connection with myself. At the time that traitors in the Senate of the United States plotted against the Government and entered into a conspiracy more foul, more execrable, and more odious than that of Catiline against the Romans I happened to be a member of that body, and, as to loyalty, stood solitary and alone among the Senators from the Southern States.

I was then and there called upon to know what I would do with such traitors, and want to repeat my reply here. I said, if we had an Andrew Jackson he would hang them as high as Haman, but as he was no more, and sleeps in his grave in his own beloved State, where traitors and treason have even insulted his tomb and the very earth that covers his remains, humble as

I am, when you ask me what I would do, my reply is, I would arrest them; I would try them; I would convict them; and I would hang them.

As humble as I am and have been, I have pursued but one, undeviating course. All that I have—life, limb, and property—have been put at the disposal of the country in this great struggle. I have been in camp, I have been in the field, I have been everywhere this great rebellion was; I have pursued it until I believe I can now see its termination. Since the world began, there has never been a rebellion of such gigantic proportions, so infamous in character, so diabolical in motive, so entirely disregardful of the laws of civilized war. It has introduced the most savage mode of warfare ever practiced upon the earth.

*   *   *   *   *   *   *

. . . I am in favor of leniency; but, in my opinion, evil doers should be punished. [" That's so! " his audience cried.] Treason is the highest crime known in the catalogue of crimes, and for him that is guilty of it—for him that is willing to lift his impious hand against the authority of the nation—I would say death is too easy a punishment. My notion is that treason must be made odious, that traitors must be punished and impoverished, their social power broken, they must be made to feel the penalty of their crime. . . .

It is not the men in the field who are the greatest traitors. It is the men who have encouraged them to imperil their lives, while they themselves remain at home expanding their means and exerting all their power to overthrow the Government. Hence I say this: " the halter for intelligent, influential traitors." But to the honest boy, to the deluded men, who have been deceived into the rebel ranks, I would extend leniency: I would say, return to your allegiance, renew your support to the Government, and become good citizens; but the leaders I would hang.

I hold, too, that wealthy traitors should be made to remunerate those men who have suffered as a consequence of their crime— Union men who have lost property, who have been driven from their homes, beggars and wanderers among strangers. It is well to talk about these things here today, in addressing the well-informed persons who compose this audience. You can to a very great extent, aid in moulding public opinion. We have put down these traitors in arms. Let us put them down in law, in public judgment, and in the morals of the world.

Throughout his speech the Vice-President was repeatedly interrupted by loud and prolonged cheers. After his concluding sentence three spontaneous cheers rent the air for Johnson. Vindictive persons who feared that Abraham Lincoln would be too lenient with Southerners wished that the Vice-President from Tennessee occupied the White House.[3]

A twentieth-century cosmopolite might react vigorously to so much speechmaking, but his ancestor in 1865 applauded and called for more. Green Clay Smith, who had served as a Union officer until his election as representative from Kentucky, supported Johnson's demand for punishment. The country from north to south, from east to west, was clad in the habiliments of mourning, he said, and those traitors—Davis, Toombs, Benjamin, and Breckinridge—were responsible. If he had his way, Smith would hang them. " Go, if you please, to the bloody grounds of Kentucky, the home of my birth and childhood, and go to that place where I played as a child, and where my mother nursed me on her knee, and listen to her story of the pleasures of five and twenty

[3] After the assassination of Lincoln the responsibilities of office subdued Andrew Johnson. In the end he accepted almost in totality Lincoln's plan for reconstructing the South. His vindictive Republican former friends turned against him and instituted congressional reconstruction. Although more rigorous than the presidential plans, it did not include hangings or the confiscation of private property. In fact congressional reconstruction, viewed from the perspective of world history, was harsh only in comparison to presidential reconstruction or to what Southerners desired. In comparison to treatment given the loser in other civil wars of the world, congressional reconstruction was lenient.

years ago, and what will you find? Desolation and ruin stare you in the face, and all at the hands of Kentucky traitors and scoundrels. Should I forgive them? "

" No! Never! " the crowd answered.

" No, my friends you have spoken aright. Never! No, never! So help me God, I will never do it. They tore from its proud mast the flag which for so long a time has proudly floated to the breeze all over this vast domain, the home of freemen, and trailed it in the dust beneath their feet; but the time is not far distant when they will hang so high their feet will never touch the ground to trample again upon that starry flag, that glorious emblem of liberty."

Smith delighted his audience by reading a report that Grant had Lee on the run. " I tell you, fellow citizens, this same little man, who is much assimilated to a bull-dog, short-legged, stout, and muscular, with a big head and bobtailed, will outrun Lee yet. . . . And there is another man, with long legs, and who is notorious for long and speedy marches, by the name of Sherman. Yes, you all know him, he is coming up at the rate of twenty knots an hour."

The amused crowd cheered Smith on. " The city of Richmond, that citadel of treason, the great central point, was taken possession of by a lot of soldiers of African descent, and led by a Dutchman. Now, where is that bragging chivalry of the South, which flattered itself that one of them could whip five Yankees, in the beginning of the war, when now fifty thousand of them run from a thousand negroes."

Smith ended his speech with a tribute to the administration and especially to Lincoln. But the insatiable people called for more. Eager hands lifted Charles S. Spencer, president of the Republican Club of New York, and voices demanded a speech. Although he praised the eloquence of preceding speakers, Spencer said the most meaningful utterance of the day came from an old Negro woman in the audience, who only a few moments before rolled her eyes heavenward and exclaimed: " Bress de Lor! De year of jubelo am come." The most signal instance of Divine justice the world has even seen, Spencer claimed, was witnessed that day by haughty, slave-driving Richmond in her occupation by a battalion of black men. " The first shot fired at Fort Sumter bore upon its felon wing the death of slavery; and today, by this great defeat of the rebel armies, and the occupation of their capital . . . this nation tears from its limbs the black sackcloth of slavery, and robes them in the pure and bridal white of universal emancipation."

And so with such orations the afternoon faded into evening in Washington. Happy crowds roamed from government building to hotel to residence, ever eager for new faces and different voices to tell them the glorious news over and over again. Repetition bothered them not at all. Listening to the speeches, the individual identified himself with victory. He became the savior of the Union, the liberator of downtrodden slaves, the avenger of God. It gave him a warm feeling, a sensation of soaring above mundane affairs, and a kinship with the Almighty.

All through the night the celebration continued. Bands serenaded Seward, Stanton, and Johnson; musicians played for their regimental commanders; householders rewarded singers with invitations to punch and dancing; and the masses watched pyrotechnic displays or gazed at illuminated buildings. Gaslights brightened Ford's and Grover's theaters and Geary's Billiard Hall, where mottoes, flags, and designs adorned the buildings. Chief Justice Salmon P. Chase lighted his dwelling and welcomed all callers. At intervals brilliant lights shot skyward from the fireworks at the Navy Yard. There had been so little time for preparation that few homeowners or businessmen were able to make the desired displays. Secretary Seward recommended that all public buildings be illuminated the following evening.

This announcement provided the excuse for many people who lined bars in saloons to make the celebration a two-day affair. Men with drinking proclivities took more than their usual quotas, and those usually sober became exuberant as toast succeeded toast. One sedate Vermonter, the chief of a government bureau, stood on the corner of F and Fourteenth streets giving away fifty-cent " shinplasters " to every passing Negro and saying with each gift: " Babylon has fallen." A more liquorish crowd was never seen in Washington than the one on the night of April 3. It was fortunate for Abraham Lincoln that he was at City Point, Virginia. He would have been serenaded hour after hour and called on for speech after speech. The enthusiasm which captured the city would have centered at the White House, had he been there, and the crowd would have taken him upon its shoulders to parade him in tribute to their victory.

(III)

OCCUPIED CITY, *April 4, 1865*

WASHINGTON

WASHINGTONIANS WHO WERE NOT suffering from hangovers or sleeping in drunken stupors arose early on April 4 to continue their celebrating. Bold headlines in the *Morning Chronicle* promised details on the occupation of Richmond, the fire, Negro troops, captured war matériel, and the reception of Federal soldiers. Avid readers sated their appetites in column after column of general and special reports.

Everyone heartily agreed with some of the ideas in the leading editorial, "The End of the Rebellion." The flight of Jefferson Davis from Richmond, the editor stated, signified the substantial, if not the final, overthrow of the Southern

Confederacy. So long as it had remained securely in Richmond, the government had possessed a local habitat; so long as General Lee had held the city and thereby protected his lines of communication, his army had been formidable; but with the fall of Richmond, the Confederacy was no longer a " belligerent " power. Although some enemy troops might retreat to the fortresses of the Alleghenies, the great military operations were ended. Only one government would control the vast area between the Atlantic and Pacific oceans. " The power and capacity of a free people, not only to develop the resources of a continent, but to protect and defend their nationality, has been indisputably demonstrated, not only at the peaceful contest of the ballot-box, but on the bloodiest and best-fought fields of battle ever known in the history of the world."

The editor would not presume to tell the Congress or the President what should be done with Southern leaders. He believed, however, that the war inculcated respect on both sides and demonstrated that valor was confined neither to the North or South, but belonged to all. Furthermore, the contest proved that the real power of a genuine democracy lay in free speech, a free press, and the education of the masses. " Had the South enjoyed these privileges, Slavery could never have endured. . . ." Though the victors were stirred to bitter feelings of hatred and revenge by the " well-authenticated statements of rebel barbarities, and of the cowardly murders and ferocious cruelties committed by the Confederate authorities on Union prisoners of war," this editor asked his readers to rise above the prejudices and passions of the hour. " The great contest is over. The Government of the United States is fully established. This result will redound to the benefit of no section, but of the whole country." And the editor concluded: " Let us not indulge in vituperation, passion, or revenge, but thank God that He has safely led us through this terrible ordeal."

These liberal and sympathetic sentiments were brushed aside by a people charmed that day with victory and with the end of a long war. Few men worked in their usual ways. Business establishments decorated their doors and windows instead of selling goods. Men mounted ladders to attire store fronts in gay bunting. Pipe fitters attached gas lines and lights to walls fronting on streets. Candles and banners were strung over avenues. Before dark Pennsylvania Avenue from the White House to the Capitol was almost covered with lights and ribbons. Patriotic organizations scoured the city for roman candles, rockets, and other fireworks. Bandsmen cleaned uniforms and polished musical instruments. Servants and householders decorated homes.

Yet even in the joy of planning for the night's festivities, some essential work was accomplished. Roscoe G. Greene, formerly a prosperous merchant of Richmond, accepted the postmastership of that city from the United States government. He left his clerkship in the United States Auditor's Office and started for the captured Confederate capital. An eminent Washington photographer took his camera and chemicals and went to Richmond to record the memorable scenes in that city. At the Sixth Street wharf stevedores loaded the *Rebecca Barton* with medical and engineering stores for the Southern city. In midafternoon she steamed away, the first ship to leave Washington for Richmond in almost four years. At the White House, Mary Todd Lincoln, who had returned from City Point, Virginia, only a few days before, packed dresses for a return trip. She arranged for Senator James Harlan, Mrs. Harlan, and their daughter Mary (who would later be married to Robert Lincoln), Senator Charles Sumner, and other dignitaries to accompany her. They planned to sail the following day for City Point, and from there to visit occupied Richmond.

In the bustle of preparation for the festive evening, individuals swapped yarns about the fleeing Confederate President. Even though not having a press agent, Brady's gymnasium made a newspaper column, where it was suggested that a corps of the splendidly conditioned runners, devotees of the physical culture program at the gymnasium, be sent after Jefferson Davis, who was too fleet of foot for ordinary racers to catch. One story claimed that doctors had advised Davis and his cabinet to leave Richmond for a tour of the mountains of Virginia and North Carolina, because too long confinement had impaired their health, and exercise in the open air was prescribed as indispensable for a restoration. No one knew where the President was headed, wags said; some thought it was through the oak clearings of the southeast and the prairies of Texas; others said a sea voyage was in prospect.

Fun-loving men wrote imaginary proclamations. One, entitled " Jeff Davis's Valedictory Proclamation," was published.

Whereas in the course of inhuman Yankee events the capital of the Confederate States of America no longer affords an eligible and healthy residence . . . I do therefore, by virtue of the power vested in my heels, proclaim my intention to travel instanter, in company with all officers of the Confederate States Government and to take up such agreeable quarters as may yet be *Granted* unto me. . . . Under the circumstances, slavery had better be abolished. The capital of the Confederacy will henceforth be found " up a stump " on the picturesque banks of the celebrated " Last Ditch." . . . It is not altogether improbable that the glorious experiment of a slaveholder's Confederacy may yet be a delusion and a snare. I have often thought so. So has General Lee, who has lately been fighting mostly for his last year's salary. The Confederate Treasury being light, I think I will take it in my valise. General Lee thinks we have a good opening before us . . . All persons having claims against this Government will please present them to A. Lincoln, Richmond, by whom all such accounts will be most cheerfully audited. . . .

The spurious proclamation went on for paragraph after paragraph. Happy Washingtonians enjoyed adding additional sentences and vied with each other in composing what they considered amusing tales about the fugitive Confederate President. Their " literary " efforts continued at early suppers, for almost everyone planned to attend the mass meeting called by the Lincoln and Johnson clubs for seven o'clock at the Patent Office building.

Before sunset the streets were crowded. Bands paraded and serenaded important officials. By dark Pennsylvania Avenue near the governmental buildings was almost impassable. Promptly at seven Secretary of the Interior Usher called the meeting to order. A band from Harewood Hospital entertained the milling audience in front of the Patent Office building. Usher introduced Judge Cartter of the Washington Superior Court. We have learned a few lessons in four years of war, the Judge shouted. We have learned " that we have a national military institution to raise up and educate traitors. . . . The flying rascal out of Richmond was one of them and his class is composed of them. I trust that this Government of ours will attach to that institution [The United States Military Academy] one additional lesson, in its course of instruction, and that is the lesson of patriotism; for I hesitate not to say that those who have been fed, clothed, and taught at the public expense, ought to stretch the rope first."

We have learned another lesson, Cartter told his now-cheering audience, that some men go to Wall Street to buy and sell the nation's life, as the Jews of old did the garments of Christ, while our sons died on battlefields. " The Jews have not been naturalized to the country, and have no real home anywhere—that's the best I can say for them," the Judge concluded; and the people, ever ready to link Jews with other scapegoats, roared and cheered.

They also applauded the saner utterances of Senator George Henry Williams of Oregon. "Let the day speedily advance," the Senator prayed, "when every American, though he be in New England, or on the great prairies of the West, or the savannahs of the South, will feel everywhere within its borders that the country is *his,* and that he belongs to the country, and that from the fulness of an appreciative heart, he can look upon every foot of American soil to which the Constitution attaches, and over which the flag waves, and say this is my country, my home, my green land forever."

Vice-President Johnson answered repeated calls for a speech. He reiterated his ideas of the day before and concluded by asking what should be done with Jefferson Davis. "Hang him," the crowd roared. "I'd hang him twenty times over," Johnson declared, "and confiscate property of the leaders to repay the losses of loyal men."

Other men spoke, one after the other. A few of them advised moderation in dealing with Southern leaders; more of them called for punishment; and all of them praised the President, the generals, and the soldiers. At last the speech-making ended, and the people could parade Pennsylvania Avenue to view the illuminated buildings with their displays and mottoes.

Every door of the Patent Office was lighted by gas jets. At the main entrance on F Street the burners were arranged in an arch to spell "Union." Garrison flags adorned the War Department, and underneath them was "The Union, it must and shall be preserved," with a papier-mâché eagle, its talons clutching a scroll inscribed "Richmond." The brilliantly lighted State Department presented two credos.

Over the east door was " Peace and good will to all nations, but no entangling alliances and no foreign intervention." The crowd cheered the one over the north door: " At home, Union is order, and order is peace. Abroad, Union is strength and strength is peace." Thousands of lights shone on flags at the Treasury Department, and transparencies over one door pictured the Currency Bureau with " U. S. greenbacks and U. S. Grant—Grant gives the greenbacks a metallic ring." Jay Cooke and Company displayed in story-high numerals, " 5-20 " and " 7-30," representing the interest and maturity of bonds. The numerals supported a banner inscribed " The Bravery of our Army, the Valor of our Navy, sustained by our Treasury, upon the faith and substance of a Patriotic People." Grover's Theater was lit by gas and Chinese lanterns, with a " victory " transparency covering the front of the building. Fireworks were shot from its roof.

More impressive than all the other buildings, the Capitol was circled from base to dome by five tiers of lights. To one standing in any part of the city, the picture looked more like a fairy scene than reality. Washington blazed with lights; roman candles, rockets, and other fireworks shot glowing streams skyward. Towering above everything in its majesty stood the Capitol, its rows of lights appearing from a distance as unbroken bands flowing upward from its pedestal to its dome, upon which the goddess of liberty reigned in simple beauty.

Every Federal building displayed some sort of decoration. Most of the stores glowed inside and out. Even in residential districts windows invited passers-by to stop and stare. Bachelor Thaddeus Stevens had his house on B Street trimmed with flags and other patriotic emblems, and soft candlelight made the display artistic and beautiful. Every window of Chief Justice Chase's residence at Sixth and E streets was adorned with variegated lights. Most popular of all with the celebrators was the brilliantly illuminated White House.   Crowds walked through the grounds, stopping to cheer the absent President, and band after band paused to serenade his wife.

For hours people walked the streets in tireless procession, singing, shouting, and exchanging congratulations. On the outskirts of the crowd ladies rode in carriages needlessly lighted by feeble lamps in a city which had turned night into day. Horsemen vainly pushed their horses against the crowd, then tethered their mounts and walked. Dancing, singing Negroes received enthusiastic applause and warm comments on the freedom of their fellow men.

Slowly the crowds on the streets thinned. Mothers took their children home to bed. Men called on important officials who were holding open house. Here and there music floated from living rooms where couples waltzed in graceful rhythm. Toasts were drunk in crowded bars. But in time Washington slept, content in the knowledge that Federal soldiers guarded occupied Richmond, and that the Union was a reality again.

RICHMOND

IN CONTRAST to what was happening in Washington, an unnatural quiet covered Richmond. At two o'clock in the morning General Shepley saw only the Federal sentinels walking their rounds in otherwise deserted streets. Those left homeless by the fire camped on vacant lots or on Capitol Square. No lights flickered from windows in the residential areas. Almost everyone in Richmond slept, exhausted in body and mind.

The thoughts of those who could not find oblivion in sleep were alien to those of celebrating Washingtonians. For most Southerners the fall of Richmond and the collapse of the Confederacy were twin tragedies. Some feared the vengeance of the North, for they knew defeated rebellious subjects had always fared poorly at the hands of the victor. Yet Southerners would not admit to rebellion. For them secession had been a legal act of a sovereign state against unheard grievances. They considered themselves Southern patriots rather than United States traitors. They admitted no guilt, and they grieved for their failure rather than for their attempt. One soldier later said: "I was willing to admit that we were whipped. . . . I was not willing to say I was sorry for what I had done, nor did I then think or believe that [the United States Government] was the best the world had ever seen; [for] four years of war against its tyranny and oppression had made deep seated prejudice, if not hatred against it. . . ." Neither did these Southerners blame God, Who in their opinion undoubtedly favored them. They, as Job of old, were being tested in defeat. Somehow they had failed the Almighty, and they must move closer to Him to prove their faith and through His grace achieve final victory over the godless Yankees. Nor would they admit that the southland was or had been a land where the cherished human freedom of its forefathers had languished. It had been a land of opportunity for all but slaves, and they had been content in the service of understanding masters. Emancipation was not worthy of serious thought, for the Negro belonged to a biologically inferior race. He neither possessed nor needed the economic, social, and political rights of the white man. Northerners—who endowed the Negro with great native virtue, who thought of him as a painted white, who did not realize that he would retrogress to barbarism without the white man's supervision—such Northerners composed a lunatic fringe of "do-gooders." Only through the institution of slavery could the Negro be saved from his tendency toward laziness, irresponsibility, and violence.

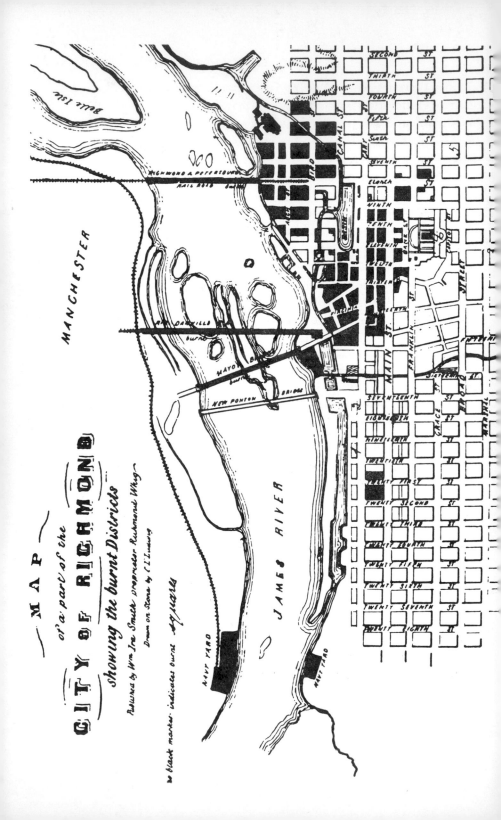

— MAP —
of a part of the
CITY OF RICHMOND
showing the burnt Districts

Published by Wm Ira Smith Proprietor Richmond Whig

Drawn on Stone by C.L.Ludwig

☞ black marks indicate burnt squares

MANCHESTER

Belle Isle

RICHMOND & PETERSBURG
RAIL ROAD

R.R. DANVILLE burnt

MAYO BRIDGE

NEW PONTOON BRIDGE

JAMES RIVER

NAVY YARD

NAVY YARD

SECOND ST
THIRD ST
FOURTH ST
FIFTH ST
SIXTH ST
SEVENTH
EIGHTH ST
NINTH
TENTH
ELEVENTH
TWELFTH
THIRTEENTH
FOURTEENTH
FIFTEENTH

CANAL ST

MAIN ST
FRANKLIN ST

SIXTEENTH ST
SEVENTEENTH ST
EIGHTEENTH
NINETEENTH
TWENTIETH
TWENTY FIRST
TWENTY SECOND ST
TWENTY THIRD
TWENTY FOURTH
TWENTY FIFTH
TWENTY SIXTH
TWENTY SEVENTH ST
TWENTY EIGHTH

GRACE ST
BROAD ST
MARSHALL

Southerners awakening in Richmond on the morning
of April 4 did admit, however, the discipline and courtesy of
both black and white Federal soldiers. Rather than destroying it, they had saved a city fired by retreating Confederates;
instead of committing rapine, they had guarded defenseless
women; in contrast to expected vandalism, they had fed the
hungry. Underneath their bright blue uniforms they seemed
as youthful and high-spirited as Confederate boys in tattered
gray. Somewhere in that distant, hated northland, mothers,
wives, and sweethearts were praying for the safety and the
souls of their men in Richmond. One Virginia girl sympa-
thized with the sleeping Yankees lying near her window.
Early risers saw others slumbering on sidewalks. Their tents
dotted Capitol Square and in suburban camps some ten
thousand Negro and white soldiers kept their peace near
a hostile city.

Both Federal and city officials surveyed the damage on
Monday, April 4. The fire had consumed the heart of Richmond's business district. Beginning at Shockoe Warehouse,
the flames had radiated on all sides, burning on the south
side of Main Street down to Jacobson's store between Fourteenth and Fifteenth streets and from there south to the
James River; on the north side of Main the ruins extended
from Mitchell and Tyler's jewelry store between Thirteenth
and Fourteenth streets to beyond Ninth, north to Bank
Street at Capitol Square and east of the square to Grace
Street. In an area bounded by Canal, Fourth and Fifteenth
streets, and the river, hardly a building remained. A block
and a half near Dibrell's Warehouse at Twenty-first Street
lay in charred ruins. Only the stone piers of Mayo's Bridge
and the two railroad trestles remained. The small navy yards
on both sides of the river were destroyed. The truce ship
William Allison and a few smaller boats were afloat. Ten
blocks on Main Street were so littered with debris that even

those most familiar with Richmond could not locate there the sites of former buildings. Fragments of brick, granite, iron, and charred timbers so cluttered cross streets that they were only vague outlines among the ruins.

The indiscriminate flames devoured stores, government buildings, hotels, banks, newspapers, and factories. More than a dozen drug stores were leveled; the Richmond, Commonwealth, Virginia, Farmers' and Traders' banks were gone; the *Examiner, Dispatch,* and *Enquirer* newspaper offices, along with those of the *Illustrated News,* the old plant of the *Literary Messenger,* the *Central Presbyterian,* and *Religious Herald* were no more; the post office, the Mechanics Institute which had housed the Confederate War Department, the architecturally beautiful state courthouse at the Franklin Street entrance to Capitol Square, the jail, and the Henrico County courthouse were destroyed. The American and Columbian hotels, many restaurants, bookstores, saloons, jewelry and grocery stores, mortuaries, flour mills, warehouses—the buildings which formerly had lined busy streets were replaced now by an amphitheater of crumbling walls and tottering chimneys. Almost twenty blocks of Richmond lay in waste of smoking ruins, blackened walls, and lonely chimneys.

Insurance offices burned with all their records complicated the accurate assessment of losses. A reporter estimated the total loss at $2,146,240, based on the low tax valuation of 1860, and this sum did not include government buildings or untaxed railroad property. In later years a student concluded that $30,000,000 was a fair estimate of the value of buildings and their contents, and of personal property lost in the fire. Bankrupted by the Confederate defeat, the insurance companies could pay no claims.

Because of its granite walls, slate roof, and iron doors the Customs House, the former Confederate treasury, was blackened with soot, but otherwise undamaged. The granite front of the Bank of the Commonwealth had become the façade of a burned-out shell. The famed Spottswood Hotel was saved only by a change in the direction of the wind. Of all the churches, only the United Presbyterian burned. Across the street from the burned church, Mrs. Stanard's house lay in charred ruins. Fortunately the fire did not reach the capitol, the governor's mansion, the city hall, or the Confederate White House; but many county, state, and Confederate records were forever lost.

The infamous (by Northern standards) Libby Prison stood surrounded by smoking ruins. In this former domicile of Union prisoners of war, Weitzel imprisoned some Confederate stragglers and deserters along with a few arrested officials. They peered through iron gratings while Federal guards apparently enjoyed the change in occupancy. Castle Thunder also remained and held Negro plunderers and looters of the preceding day.

In one form or another all the residents of Richmond suffered some loss. Approximately four-fifths of the stores in the city were destroyed by the fire or appropriated by the pillagers. Burned bridges, wrecked railroads, and river obstructions left the city to be supplied by wagons and carts. Only the Federal army possessed these in sufficient numbers to transport supplies in quantity. But ample provisions would have been of little benefit to a people without purchasing power. Confederate and state paper currency, bonds, and bank deposits were almost worthless. Negro and white boys picked Confederate bills from the streets and peddled them to Yankee soldiers. Unless one held gold or silver coins, Federal greenbacks, or property for barter, he could buy nothing. Formerly wealthy men were penniless. Burned factories and stores could not furnish employment. Broken rails and dislocated trade limited the activities of solvent enterprises and the employment of laborers.

The poverty and suffering of so many people touched General Weitzel. Families in fashionable residences and in shanty houses needed food. The general agreed to supply all who would take a simple oath of allegiance to the United States and apply for subsistence. No one knew the number of inhabitants remaining in Richmond. One reporter estimated the civilian population at twenty thousand, with half of the total Negro, but this guess was low. Other than a few small fish caught by Negroes, there was nothing for sale in the markets.

The poor of all classes did not hesitate to apply to the occupying army for relief. Pride did not deter the hungry whites from the slum areas, or the free Negroes, or the ex-slaves from pleading and begging for help from the Yankees. The *New York Times* correspondent reported that the most pathetic scene in Richmond was the thousands of destitute people begging at the provost marshal's office for provisions.

The formerly wealthy were reluctant, but many of them applied, also. The capitol and city hall were filled with people of all ages, colors, and sexes, with baskets in hand and appeal written on their faces. Only a few aristocratic males joined the throng; the others passed the burden and humiliation to their wives. Some of the latter persuaded servants or former slaves to make the appeal. But other aristocratic women dressed in their best, veiled their faces, and joined the lines. Almost invariably Federal officers spotted them and extended them unusual consideration. Constance Cary saw many of the formerly wealthy class, stately women with heads held high and with sad eyes underneath heavy veils, asking for food and justifying their act by the hunger of their children.

The provisions they received were not the dainties they had anticipated. The thought of drawing rations from Yankees shocked two teen-aged girls, but an older woman of their household exclaimed: " I'll take anything 1 can get from the Yankees. They haven't had any delicacy of feeling in taking everything we've got. I'm going for rations." She persuaded the mother of one of the girls to join her. Although unwilling to make the venture, the girls expected sugar, tea, and other luxuries. The women returned, each holding a large dried codfish and an inch-thick slab of fat bacon about half the size of a handkerchief. They sliced the bacon and prepared a meal with some fried potatoes and boiled dried peas. The codfish were hung from a window because of their odor, and pieces of them were used from time to time.

The Federal commissary could supply neither necessities in sufficient quantity nor even a few delicacies to a city at least one-third of whose citizens needed aid. Agents of the Christian Commission of the army, the Sanitary Commission, and privately supported Northern humanitarian organizations studied the situation and established relief stations. Before many days passed, these Northern public and private philanthropies were issuing thousands of rations. Most provisions were basic: meat, meal, and flour; but there was also some coffee, tea, and sugar. General Weitzel approved the appointment of a citizens' committee in Richmond to aid in distributing relief to destitute families.

The General took a pardonable pride in reporting his successes. His army captured approximately five hundred cannon and five thousand muskets, and the total of captured matériel was enormous. There were three hundred damaged but usable railroad cars and thirty engines. More than one thousand Confederate soldiers were captured, and five thousand wounded Southerners in Richmond hospitals fell under

Union control. The latter were a problem because of limited supplies, but for the first time in years they received medicines which had been denied them by the blockade. A few small boats and the unfinished ram *Texas*, with her engines intact, were secured in the river.

Weitzel's engineers started a pontoon bridge on the river from Seventeenth Street. Within two days it was completed. Naval engineers worked around the clock to remove obstructions and torpedoes from the James. The stone piers of the Danville Railroad bridge remained, and workmen laid a superstructure on them to support tracks. Work progressed so rapidly that postal agents anticipated that the mails would be restored quickly. Commissary officers knew that an adequate supply of provisions could soon be brought into the city.

Under direction of the provost marshal city firemen, assisted by Negro laborers, pulled down walls left blackened and dangerous by the fire. The army employed white and colored workmen to clear the debris from city streets. Although it would require days to complete this work, before night Main Street was again passable. Weitzel and his staff took pride in the fact that Federal soldiers had not started but had stopped the fire. A number of Richmond citizens complimented the General on his achievement and at last extended greetings to Union soldiers. Some owners of vacant lots rented them to Northern sutlers whose wares attracted individuals with money or barterable commodities. Reconciliation and reconstruction had begun.

General Weitzel made rules to govern the occupied city. All bars and saloons were closed and penalties were prescribed for selling intoxicating drink to civilians or soldiers. The provost marshal registered adult white male inhabitants, requiring them to give their names, ages, occupations, and places of residence. All of them were urged but not forced to take an oath of allegiance to the United States. Permits to enter and leave the city were granted to loyal persons and to those taking the oath. Farmers were encouraged to bring provisions into Richmond for sale. At the same time martial law remained in force, and such acts as disrespect to the United States flag, interference with Federal soldiers on duty, and stealing brought speedy arrest to the offenders. Requests for guards were freely granted to the fearful. Complaints against soldiers for unauthorized entry and search of houses received prompt attention. Over and over officers cautioned their men to be circumspect in performing their duties. Those soldiers who disregarded the orders were usually intoxicated, for notwithstanding the destruction of whiskey and strict orders prohibiting the sale of any liquor, alcoholic drinks could be obtained. But the promptness with which the military investigated complaints gave the Richmond people confidence.

Captured tobacco and other commodities were labeled with the place and time of seizure, condition, and amount. Whenever ownership by the Confederacy was established, the material became Federal property. But Weitzel ordered the restoration of private property to its rightful owners. In case of disputed ownership, claims were received and settlement was made at once, or final adjudication came later in court decisions. Thomas Jones, George B. Stephens, John Gibbon, and other people filed claims and declared their boxes of tobacco had been broken open by the mob and their contents scattered. Federal soldiers gathered loose tobacco and stored it in Ludlam and Watson's warehouse. Because of the impossibility of identifying loose tobacco, ownership could not be established.

But inanimate property did not give General Weitzel the difficulty that human visitors from the North brought him. Richmond exerted magnetic appeal for reporters who were anxious to pen pictures of the occupied city and its inhabitants for readers in Northern cities. Individuals with relatives below the Potomac, families with men now stationed in Richmond, and the merely curious—all tried to visit the former Confederate capital. Richmond hotels, restaurants, and food supplies were inadequate to take care of these tourists. Yet beginning on April 4, their numbers increased so rapidly that Weitzel eventually had to refuse passes to all except those having permits from the President, the Secretary of War, General Grant, or departmental commanders.

Most trying of all were the high Federal officials who arrived unannounced in the city which had so recently been the enemy capital and was naturally still filled with Confederate sympathizers. Not knowing of their plans, Weitzel could neither meet them nor provide them military protection. The first to arrive was Tennessee-born Vice-Admiral David Glasgow Farragut, who at the beginning of the war had moved from Norfolk, Virginia, to New York State, and who had become the most famous Federal naval commander. In 1866 he was to be rewarded for his loyalty and service by promotion to admiral, the first full admiral in American history. But long before dawn on April 4, 1865, he collected a party for a trip to the fallen capital. With Brigadier General George H. Gordon, Mrs. Gordon, more officials, and more of their ladies, he left Norfolk on the *City of Hudson* and arrived at Varina Landing below Richmond at daybreak. From there the visitors rode by wagon and horseback into the city. For a few hours they toured Richmond and called on Weitzel and other military officers. Then as they sailed away from Rockett's on the truce ship *William Allison*, they met Rear Admiral Porter and President Lincoln ascending the river.

Newspaper reporters had come to the city even before the

President or the admirals. Some of them moved in with the army of occupation, and others hastened down from Northern cities to cover the climactic events. Eventually the important Northern metropolitan dailies boasted of at least one correspondent in Richmond. The stories they filed included descriptions of the city and its citizens, of the attitudes of Southern white people and Negroes, and of what the Federal soldiers were doing in Richmond. Since fleeing Confederates and advancing Federals had little time to record events, these reporters' stories are invaluable to us now. Undoubtedly many newspapermen wrote exaggerated accounts for home consumption, and even imaginary ones; but most of the correspondents of the city dailies were conscientious in their work.

The Cincinnati *Gazette* reporter entered Richmond on the New Market Road, a route of the occupying Federal army. He saw the green wheat fields and the delicate peach blossoms among pale green leaves, and they impressed him. His wagon left the country road, and the wheels bumped along the rough pavement of the streets of the city's outskirts. Squalid houses, tow-headed children, all the poverty and degradation of the outcasts of a great city came into his view, and other than these poor people he saw little of interest except flagstaffs protruding from the miserable hovels and flying the Stars and Stripes. He described the army wagons which rattled over the streets, the files of Negro soldiers that moved quietly on the pavements, the masses of former slaves who looked on in high glee; and he wrote that occasionally a Confederate soldier in gray passed unnoticed.

He told how the streets were littered with broken brick, and how on the left toward the river there stretched an expanse of crumbling walls and smoking ruins. In the James River parts of the hulls of two ironclad ships showed above the water, and above the hulls stood the piers of what had been a bridge. North of Main Street, the state capitol and the magnificent equestrian statue of George Washington dominated the city.

At the Spottswood Hotel " Agate " secured a suite with parlor and bedroom. A Negro bellboy took his baggage, polished his dusty boots, and promised to wash and iron his clothing within six hours. All the servants of the Spottswood were former slaves and were well trained in their duties. They moved with " all deliberate speed," but they appeared happy in their work. The hotel was well scrubbed, but the carpets showed wear and the furnishings were old.

The *New York Times* correspondent spent hours on the streets of Richmond observing the people. He saw many individuals of the poorer class, but their expressions indicated native intellect and their attempted gentility in dress told him that their want and hunger were of recent origin. The number of " poor-white trash " was fewer than the reporter had expected. He saw some women groping piteously in smouldering ruins and a few laborers loitering listlessly on the streets. The fire, the poor whites complained to him, showed the abundance of provisions within Richmond, the greed of speculators who had held food for exhorbitant prices, and the corruption of avaricious Confederate leaders. None of the poor people were reticent in voicing their dislike of Negroes and they hesitated even less in condemning their " late Confederate masters." No man or woman uttered a word to him in defense of Jefferson Davis, of the Confederate cabinet members, or of the Confederate generals. In a sulky manner these people admitted their pleasure in being under the old flag again.

He saw several ladies of the upper class approach the military officer in charge at city hall. Their attire was genteel and in good taste, and their faces were so closely veiled as to defy the gaze of the keenest eye. " They spoke in such tremulous tones when giving their names as to cause us to suspect their names as foreign to them as the hunger they now sought to appease had been in days gone by." The *Times* correspondent also stated that many a wealthy Richmond family had large supplies of food on hand. These stores had been accumulated even though Confederate officials had made repeated appeals for all patriots to give food for the army.

It gratified another reporter to see no foolish displays by Richmonders of spite toward the invaders, such as by keeping out of sight or by unladylike behavior on the streets. Although General Weitzel ordered people to remain indoors except for necessary movement, many citizens did appear in the city. In the almost unharmed aristocratic residential area, ladies frequently appeared in public. Passing houses there an observer noticed scores of pretty faces in sight at the windows or not too sedulously hidden among the curtains and drapes.

One reporter told his Ohio readers: " It may interest ladies to know—as another triumph of their triumphant sex— that the fashions were not blockaded." He did not see the little three-cornered, cockleshell abomination of a spring bonnet, so fashionable in New York; but there were plenty of last winter's jaunty, plumed hats, with short coquettish veils. Kid gloves were common, dainty gaiter boots abounded, and the reporter admitted: " Watchful that I am, I was guilty of seeing above them white hose surrounding more than one pair of pretty ankles." Four-fifths of the wealthy ladies wore black dresses to mourn the loss of relatives or to lament the Yankee occupation of Richmond.

Many poorer women wore dresses " that certainly came out of the Ark." " I saw more tawdry calico in a half hour's walk," a correspondent wrote, " than one could see all day on Broadway." Many of the poor creatures, he continued, who were evidently struggling to be respectable, " were out, this warm, sunny afternoon, sweltering in furs. Everything else about them was cheap and shabby; but the furs served at least to show that they had seen better days."

The attire of Southern men received scant attention from the reporters. In the main, they described Richmond males as dressed in styles a little antiquated. Apparently some were wearing out their old clothes, but there was no actual shabbiness in the aristocratic areas.

Some members of the upper class were described as bitter at the burning of Richmond, and they blamed General Ewell for it. Many of them had suffered heavy losses in buildings and merchandise. The feeling against Jefferson Davis was intense and seemed to be increasing. One reporter believed the former President would be lynched if he returned immediately to Richmond. On Broad Street a party of Richmond boys and young men walked from block to block singing, " We'll Hang Jeff Davis to a Sour Apple Tree." On the other hand there was respect for General Lee, respect mixed with veneration. " The citizens say that Lee did the best he could," the *Times* correspondent reported, " but that Jeff Davis is a scoundrel. It is reported that . . . he took with him three hundred thousand dollars in gold, and that this amount is not near all the gold he has. It is perfectly astonishing how bitter the feeling against him is." Members of the former ruling class claimed that Richmond should have been given up months ago, for that would have permitted Lee to join General Johnston, to crush Sherman, and then to turn on Grant. However, they knew that the Confederacy had received her death blow in Lee's defeat at Petersburg.

Many of the reporters agreed that Richmond without her ruins would be an attractive city. Few people in the North could imagine the misery and actual suffering, one writer stated, of families which a few days ago had been affluent and had led in making the city one of fashion and gaiety. Many well-dressed persons walking the streets were hungry and ashamed to admit it, this writer added. The " poor white trash " boldly asked for what they wanted, and got it; but the formerly comfortably situated aristocrats concealed their sufferings, and suffered more for doing so. The only saving grace of the white trash, the reporter concluded, was their rejoicing over their release from the " tyranny of Jeff Davis."

Some of the Northern observers stimulated home-town anger by their descriptions of Richmond prisons. Libby and Castle Thunder were said to be cesspools where patriotic Federal prisoners of war had endured inhuman treatment. Chains and ankle irons invoked sympathy for slaves from the reporters, and eulogies for the liberating forces. In the county jail, between fifty and sixty men, women, and children had gone without food for days and had existed in filthy stalls. One little girl of eight claimed she was in jail for stealing bread for her ill and hungry mother, and the records substantiated her story. Other prisoners were also accused of no more than petty larcenies. Major Stevens released them all.

Reporters of the Northern press could not refrain from making fun of Davis and the Confederacy. The Philadelphia *Press* printed an imaginary obituary from the destroyed *Examiner*: " Died, suddenly, at the late residency of his father, J. Davis, of strangulation, The Southern Confederacy. No funeral." According to the Washington *Chronicle*, the new " Union paper at Petersburg, *Grant's Petersburg Progress*," listed under " auction sales " the following advertisement: " To be sold very cheap (if not badly sold already), all that singularly ineligible and worthless property known as, The Southern Confederacy. For particulars, apply to Jefferson Davis. . . . Liberal terms to agents of Maximilian,

Louis Napoleon, or Victoria." The Washington *National Republican* referred to "Old Joe Mayo," mayor of Richmond for thirteen years, as an "old brandy toper." He professed love for the Union in 1861 but became a great rebel, the newspapers continued, and the "drunken old scoundrel should at least be deprived of his office."

Northern correspondents, however, were in general remarkably kind in their comments about most Southerners, and almost maudlin in their sympathy for the Southern aristocrats. One reporter saw only two men in Richmond with decent-looking horses. "Poor mules tottered on spavined bones under petty loads of forage and meal; horses pulled and tugged at 500 pounds of flour, with their shaggy coats stuck to their ribs like kid gloves over a bony hand, offering every facility for the study of the osteology of the horse." Broken windowpanes in the best dwellings were covered with squares of rough boards or sheets of newspapers.

Members of the upper classes bemoaned their fate. They resented the necessity for intermingling with the strange, incongruous throng which lined up for commissary stores; they resented their proximity to the "coarse, rude and vulgar, and the Negroes who had left their masters in their first taste of freedom." Girls of aristocratic families, who had never been taught a profession, realized that Negro maids, cooks, and laundresses were better prepared to support themselves than they were. "Unless I can get to work and make some money," one lady declared, "I must stay indoors for decency's sake." She padded her shoes with paper to keep tender skin from touching the pavement. Some satisfaction came to these women through dressing in black for mourning and through veiling their faces against the stares of Yankee men. Federal officers accepted the veils with chivalry and amusement. Pretty Mary Triplett had her veil whipped away by a gust of wind and blown to the feet of a handsome young Northern officer. He picked up the veil, covered his eyes with his cap and offered it to Mary. She accepted it without acknowledgment, but afterward the memory of the officer lingered. Ladies, and especially unattached girls, made a show of fastening window blinds, but soldiers saw many sparkling eyes close to the small openings. Whenever a Confederate in gray uniform passed by, the blinds flew open as a gesture of admiration.

Even aristocrats proved to be resourceful in this critical period. A little flour, sugar, and shortening produced cookies which Federal soldiers bought. Almost always there was a spare room to rent in a big house, and officers were searching for quarters. The rumor spread that having a Yankee officer in a household guaranteed protection from imaginary lustful soldiers, and then the doors flew open. One widow presented her roomer with her husband's sabre and belt. Advance rent paid for the necessities of life.

Although fears of rapine subsided with the disciplined behavior of white and Negro soldiers, Southern ladies still found excuse for protest. Coins, medals, and papers disappeared from the state library. Part of the library stairway railings were taken for souvenirs, and all the captured Federal flags on display were removed. Colored soldiers sat and swiveled in the speaker's chair of the Hall of Delegates. Negro civilians made merry on the hitherto forbidden grounds of Capitol Square, and the streets swarmed with Negro soldiers in blue, followed by admirers of their own race decked in looted jewelry and pilfered dresses. To cap all humiliations a white girl appeared on the streets wearing a dress made from a United States flag. This display was resented, not so much for its disrespect to the flag, but as an insult to the Confederacy.

There were scores of feminine trivialities. Women continued to patch and mend and make do with old clothes.

Eyebrows lifted to read of a reward for the return of $185,000 in bonds, for many of the securities listed were of Northern railroads and cities. The owner received just punishment in his loss because he should have invested in Southern securities. Some people gained satisfaction in telling and repeating macabre stories. One little girl did not weep because the Yankees came. She clapped her hands and danced with joy. " The Yankees have come! And now I shall have something to eat," she cried. " I'm going to have pickles and molasses and oranges and cheese and nuts and candy until I have a fit and die." And she made friends with some Yankee soldiers who refused her nothing. She stuffed her little tummy, and the next afternoon her cold body was buried in Hollywood Cemetery. A lady had rushed up Franklin Street on April 3 to get a small vial of paregoric for an ill servant. " Look at this," she said, holding up a bottle containing no more than a tablespoonful of medicine. " Richmond is in flames and I had to pay five dollars for this." In less than an hour the flames had destroyed the druggist's well-stocked pharmacy.

Good aristocrats tried to explain the riot and pillage of the previous day. Guilt, they claimed, lay with the Negroes, the foreigners in the city, and the poor whites. Above all Confederate soldiers, even stragglers in uniform, could not be guilty of looting. Not so, came the replies in letters to newspapers. " I saw hundreds of soldiers and stragglers roaming the streets of Richmond," one man wrote. " I saw soldiers break into stores of honorable men, I saw them break the doors and windows of merchants on Cary, Main, and other streets and take jewelry, boots, and shoes without aid or pressure from the foreign element." It was true, the writer continued, that some common whites and Negroes did enter the stores broken open by Confederate soldiers, but in the main they took only provisions to sustain

life. The real damage was done, he concluded, by stragglers
and thieves of the Confederate army.

The Negroes

The Negroes of Richmond interested Northern visitors
and were an enigma to Southerners. One Northern reporter
found no evidence of Negro leadership in the riot nor any
indication that they had behaved as badly as the whites.
Most colored people remained with their late masters, but
they knew they were free and chuckled over the thought.
They demanded pay for their work and their first concern
was for schools, for they believed the Yankees would teach
them to read and write. Few former slaves understood the
meaning of freedom. " All I know," a hefty man said to his
companion, " it don't take no passes now to go around
nowhar." They knew, too, that walking in Capitol Square
and smoking cigars in the capitol building were no longer
forbidden. All of them had a " vague sort of jubilant feeling
about being free" without realizing the responsibilities
attached to their new state.

They proclaimed undying love for the Yankees. They
cheered the flag, listened to the bands, and praised all Federal
men in uniform. Negro soldiers were always cause for affec-
tionate demonstrations, and ex-slaves told reporters that the
" rebel" attempt to arm Negroes failed—only slaves forced
into companies had donned Confederate uniforms.

On the afternoon of April 4 more than a thousand
Negroes congregated in Capitol Square. They strolled around
with their curious eyes fixed on Federal soldiers, or they
huddled in groups on the ground, basking in the warm sun,
their eyes following every colored soldier with obvious admiration. Their happiness was unmistakable to a reporter

who overheard a man say: " We-uns kin go jist anywhar—don't keer for no pass—go when yer want'er. Golly! de kingdom hab kim dis time for sure—dat ar what am promised in de generations to dem dat goes up tru great tribulations."

Negroes dressed in blue coats and gray, in faded finery, in butternut and nondescript colors, and in clothing of uncouth shape and fashionable cut; field hands and favored house servants jostled together, laughing, joking, shaking hands, and exchanging congratulations. " Prayers is answered "; " Massa Jeff has a very sudden call down souf"; " De Yankees at last has gone and cum." These and similar expressions filled the air. Poor souls, a correspondent exclaimed, they glory in new-found liberty without realizing that they must work energetically to prove their right to its enjoyment, and " like all other sons of men, they must buy their own experience."

The *New York Times* reporter interviewed a dozen Negro men. None of them looked forward to a simple life of ease. They wanted to work for wages, but " not for none of dis yer money which ain't werf nuffin, but de money dat you has. Dis chile'd like to hab a heap o'dat," a sturdy Negro said as he crumpled and threw down a handful of Confederate bills.

Negroes were working. Six hundred men employed by the Federal quartermaster cleared the docks and collected abandoned naval and ordnance stores. Other hundreds unloaded Federal ships, raked, shoveled, and carted away debris. Numbers of colored women agreed to cook and wash for Northern officers. A Northern observer wondered why they were so plump and well fed while white women were lean and hungry looking. He concluded that the cooks had got the pick of food in undersupplied, wartime Richmond.

The demands of some ex-slaves angered their former masters. A committee of three ex-slaves from one household informed the master that all Negroes were free but that they would continue working for him if he would pay them in Federal greenbacks. The *Tribune* correspondent suggested that the "appointment of committees [by the Negroes] was a distinctive feature of enlightened communities, and in any case indicated a very high order of civilization and a capacity for self-care." The irate master replied: "Well I told the whole crew to go to hell, and they left; its my opinion they'll all get there soon enough."

The enjoyment of witnessing the autocratic white discomfort in the new order motivated the concoction of many stories of doubtful authenticity. A widely circulated one concerned J. Morris Chester, a well-dressed, well-educated, and respectable-looking Negro reporter. Morris studied a statue of Washington in the capitol rotunda; looked into the former Confederate house and senate chambers; noted the plain pine desks and split-bottom chairs, the oil paintings on the walls, the homemade rag carpets, the numerous spittoons, the desks filled with unofficial resolutions and unpassed bills, and the stocks of poorly printed and loosely bound public documents piled near the walls. He strolled into the house chamber, seated himself in the speaker's chair, and began to write an article for the Philadelphia *Press*.

Presently one Lieutenant Butler, a Confederate recently captured but paroled, saw the Negro. "Assuming a plantation air," he shouted: "Get out of there you damned nigger." Morris continued his writing for the *Press*. The angry Southerner showered epithets on him, but Morris did not move. "At last Lieutenant Butler thought it wise, after the established plantation fashion, to proceed further; and with renewed orders to the 'damned nigger' to get out, he undertook to seize him by the collar.

"In an instant the Negro Chester straightened up out of the chair of the Speaker of the House of Delegates of the ancient commonwealth of Virginia and duly mindful of the motto of the state, dealt a splendid right-hander full between Butler's eyes, which sent the rebel sprawling down the aisle. Morris took his seat again. Butler recovered and ran scream-ing to the nearest white officer; 'Lend me your sword till I cut the damned nigger's heart out.'

"'I'll do nothing of the sort,'" replied the officer (to be sure he was a Yankee if not from Boston itself). 'But if you want to try a fair fight, I'll have a ring made for you here, and see that there's no interference. You'll get more dam-nably thrashed,' he pleasantly added, 'than ever you were, in your life.'" Lieutenant Butler hesitated but decided it wise to retire with his swollen eye, "and the Negro wrote on, in the chair of the Speaker of the House of Delegates of the State of Virginia."

Did it really happen, or was Senator Charles Sumner thus avenged in print for the beating he had received in an earlier decade from Congressman Preston Brooks, who had acted in retaliation for Sumner's criticisms of Brook's uncle, Senator Andrew Pickens Butler of South Carolina? No one knows. In a condensed account of the incident the Philadel-phia *Press* referred to "Rollin" as its Negro reporter in Richmond.

In the small plantation house, Rosewood, near the city limits, Emma Mordecai faced the new order. After turning back the day before in her attempt to enter Richmond, she and her two female relatives tossed the night away in restless fear. On the morning of April 4 they dressed with unusual care and sat down to knit. Young Massie's running off with-out permission was the first act of insubordination by any of their slaves. Adult Cyrus went to work in the field that morning, but Emma doubted that he would labor long.

The house was closely shut, but the clatter of hoofs in the yard made its occupants jump in fright. A Negro dragoon, fully armed, galloped around the house until another near the road ordered him away. Emma rejoiced at the escape and discovered herself less terrified than she had expected at the " awful sight " of a Negro soldier.

She returned to her knitting. About eleven o'clock the dread sound of hoofs returned. Emma went to the door and saw an " insolent looking Negro, dirty and ragged," sitting bareback on a horse.

" You got any saddle here? " he asked. " If you have, han' it out."

" Mary," Emma called to a Negro girl, " go to the field and get Cyrus."

" If it's de man dat was plowing," the soldier said, " he told me der was a saddle here. I done got his horse an' now I want de saddle, so han' it out and be quick 'bout it."

" Have you any paper or order to get these things? " Emma asked.

" No, but I got orders to take ev'y horse and saddle out-side de lines."

" Is there any officer with you? "

" Yes," the Negro replied, " yonder de sergeant."

Emma saw two other Negro soldiers, mounted and armed, drawn up close to the vegetable garden fence. She handed over the saddle, which the Negro put on the horse in great haste and then galloped away.

Emma decided to protest the seizure. She and two slave girls, Mary and Georgiana, started for nearby Camp Lee. Before she reached the outer picket line, she saw Negro soldiers commanded by a white officer moving a cannon from an abandoned Confederate battery. Emma informed the officer of her purpose, and he advised her to seek redress from General Draper at the camp headquarters.

The courteous captain offered the use of his horse to Emma, telling her that the animal was a very gentle creature.

Emma declined, and although the officer insisted, he respected her wishes and rode slowly by her side. His pleasant talk and gentlemanly manner impressed Emma. He dismounted at each of the little streams which crossed the road and assisted her to cross. Although his men turned off to another road with the cannon, he accompanied her to General Draper's headquarters. Finding out that the Captain was Irish, Emma expressed herself freely and told him that his kindness almost enabled her to obey the command to "love your enemies." She rejoiced that he was not a Northerner, for she disliked being indebted to a Yankee.

"I sympathize with your feelings," he said, "but please hide them in talking to General Draper. He is not a member of the regular army, and is something of a fanatic."

Emma found the general a "sleek, dapper, unmilitary looking man." However, he received her politely and offered her his chair, which was the only one in the tent. He assured her that the conduct of the Negro soldiers was against regulations. Since they probably belonged to the Fifth Massachusetts colored cavalry, she should see Colonel Adams, identify the horse and saddle, and the Colonel would return them to her. Emma refused to wander in a camp filled with "black and insolent negroes" and requested permission to return home. Unfortunately, Draper said, he was not allowed to pass anyone outside the city limits without a permit from the provost marshal's office. He could, however, allow her to go into the heart of Richmond and assured her she would be subject to no rude treatment.

Emma found a bright side to necessity. In Richmond she might see the slave George, who went in the day before with the mule and cart. She moved through the camp with its "black and blue" Negro soldiers and had never felt so "majestically and proudly defiant."

The walk from the site of present-day Broad Street Station into the center of Richmond seemed interminable to her. There were Yankee officers galloping down Broad Street on fine horses, the sidewalks were filled with people she had never seen, and Emma felt that she was in a foreign city. Turning south from Broad, she stepped carefully on pavements covered with broken or powdered glass and avoided the rough boards that covered open doorways and windows. On Ninth Street the curb was ankle deep in Confederate papers. Charred piles littered the street. Everywhere there was rubbish and disorder. The once beautiful capitol grounds looked filthy; they were thronged with native and Northern Negroes, with Federal officers riding carelessly on the grass, with a few white women, and with many troubled Richmond citizens en route to the provost marshal's office. All these native citizens " looked disconsolate, desolate and defiled." Emma found the marshal's office in the Virginia senate chamber. She spoke to one of the two officers seated at a desk and asked him for General Manning.

" I am he," the youthful officer replied. Emma requested the right to leave the city and to take the mule, cart, and George with her if they could be found. She also reported the theft of her horse and saddle. Manning told her that General Draper should have attended to the soldiers, but he did write the pass for her.

Emma found her Richmond relatives safe and unharmed. A Northern officer was rooming with them. He was most polite, a cousin reported, and his presence guaranteed protection for them and the house. As Emma and the slave girls left to hunt for George, she heard resounding cheers. " Abe Lincoln is coming," a man told her. " Then, it's time for me to get out," Emma replied. She spotted George at the Ninth Street pump watering the mule, and ran to him. He was sufficiently tipsy to be foolish and headstrong, but said he wanted to go home. They drove away with the mule walking a snake's path and George complaining that it was "Miss Emma's talking" and not whiskey which made him drive so poorly.

"At the outer picket post," Emma wrote later, ". . . we were rudely halted by a powerful, ruffianly negro picket, the blackest man I ever saw (it is usually remarked that these negro troops are the blackest of their race ever seen here) who demanded the pass. He held it upside down, and then sideways, and at last found the right way, and after pretending to read it for an immense time, returned it to me saying in his horrid voice, 'It's all right, but you must take it to the Lieutenant over yonder.' This was some distance back, so I got out and walked there, telling George to follow me, but he was too tipsy to be obedient. Well, the Lieut. (a white man) examined it and kept it, saying he had to show it, and I would not need it. I walked back to the cart, climbed in, and at last got George to start again. Meanwhile, the Black Ruffian was extremely insolent to me. I was indignant, not frightened, and treated him with sovereign contempt and coolness. As we drove off and had got at least thirty yards from him, I said speaking to myself, 'They are all as ill-bred as old Lincoln himself.'"

To Emma's astonishment, the guard yelled after her to halt. "Drive on, George," she said. "He has no right to stop us." George did drive on until the picket leveled his musket and cocked it. The two slave girls jumped from the cart and ran toward home.

"Go on, George," Emma commanded. "He won't shoot."

But George was too afraid to obey. "I seen too much ob dey carryin's on in town."

The soldier approached. "What's dat you said 'bout Lincoln?"

Emma did not answer and the question was repeated.

By this time fright had sobered George, who said: " I ain't hear her say nothin' 'bout Lincoln today." The guard "cursed" Emma.

"And suppose I were to tell you what I said about Lincoln. Would you shoot me, or stick your bayonet in me? "

" You haven't got things here no longer as you did," the guard answered. " Don't you know dat? "

Finally the Negro soldier allowed George to drive on, and Emma reached home without further incident. In retrospect, she was astonished at her own coolness, angry but not frightened. The day's venture and the assurances of the Irish captain that neither theft nor assault would be tolerated by the army, brought her peace and tranquillity.

The Mordecai Negroes promised to remain on the farm, and they did remain for a time. Later Cyrus refused to work. " Aren't you going to work anymore? " Emma inquired.

" Not 'til I know who I gwine to work for," he answered.

" Wouldn't you as soon work for your mistress as for anyone else, if she pays you? "

" I onderstands Missus Mordecai ain't got nothin' to compensate with."

" But she would have, if you and the others on the place made a crop."

" Dat don't seem right ter me," the former slave replied. " Seems lak we'uns do all the wuck and gits a part. Der ain't goin' ter be no more Master and Mistress, Miss Emma. All is equal. I done hear it from de cotehouse steps."

" Cy, do you expect to continue to live on Mrs. Mordecai without working for her? "

" Yes," he answered, " until I see how things is gwine to wuck. All de land belongs to de Yankees now, and dey gwine to divide it out 'mong de colored people. Besides, de kitchen ob de big house is my share. I help built hit."

Emma turned to young Mary. " Are you glad to be free? "

"No Mam," she repeated. "I just as leave be a slave as not." But within a few days, Mary departed in the night to her new-found freedom, never to return. So did Cyrus and his family, and even George, who had been so anxious to return a few days before.

The sudden and unannounced departure of domestic slaves hurt many sensitive women. One young matron cried herself to sleep on the disappearance of the slave with whom she had been raised and with whom she had shared most of her experiences of life. The young mistress had not realized— as so many Southerners had not—the longing of the Negro to attain human dignity. On the other hand, Northern visitors in Richmond could not understand the abiding affection of some of the former slaves for their former masters. At times Negro women, who found work with greater ease than many an aristocratic white man, returned to familiar houses and gave their former mistresses two, three, or five dollars in greenbacks.

Yet many ex-slaves became disillusioned with freedom. A white man working in his garden near Emma Mordecai's home overheard a passing Negro soliloquizing: "Dis what you call freedom! No wuck ter do, and got ter feed and clothe yourself!"

The Northerner did bring the Negro schools. Adults and children trooped to the mysterious places to learn the meaning of symbols. Their longing for education was misunderstood by Southerners, confident that the "biologically inferior" Negro should be content as the mudsill of an "Aryan civilization" and many Southerners reacted to the Negroes' efforts by manufacturing cynical stories. A neighbor of Miss Mordecai met a Negro girl on her way to school. "What are you studying?" he asked. "Dis here book," and she handed him a French grammar. He returned it and said, "That is a very suitable book for you to study."

LINCOLN

THE JOY OF EDUCATED and illiterate Negroes in Richmond knew no bounds on April 4 with the visit to that city of Abraham Lincoln. For more than a week the President's headquarters had been on the *River Queen,* anchored in the James River off City Point, Virginia. Every day the tall, stooping man walked down the gangplank to talk with soldiers in camp, to visit the sick, and to inspect the Federal fortifications. There he and his wife were reunited with their son Robert, a recently appointed captain on Grant's personal staff. On March 27 the President conferred with Grant and Sherman. Five days later Mrs. Lincoln left for Washington to assemble dignitaries there for a return trip to City Point. Young Thomas, whom Lincoln had nicknamed " Tadpole " as a baby because of his abnormally large head, remained with his father.

Lincoln was boyish in his enthusiasm during these last days of the war. From day to day he followed the progress of Grant at Petersburg. As reports mounted, his faith in immediate success increased. Some people claimed Lincoln left Washington to avoid congressmen or perhaps a forthcoming victory celebration; others said that after four years of trial he should be present for events which would make a reality of his dream—the restoration of the Union. On April 3 he visited conquered Petersburg. Back at City Point that night, he conferred with Admiral Porter and planned to enter Richmond the next day.

The next morning a flotilla composed of Porter's flagship, the *Malvern,* the *River Queen* with the President on board, and the *Bat,* moved up the James. Porter's boats had swept the river of torpedoes but had cleared only a narrow channel through river obstructions just below Richmond. One after another the vessels grounded as they manoeuvered to find the channel. Lincoln, Tad, Porter, and a detachment of guards transferred to a twelve-oared barge, and the oarsmen pulled against the current.

About eleven o'clock [1] they pulled into Rockett's Landing near Thirty-first and Main streets. Nearby twelve Negroes were digging behind a small house. Their leader, an old man, shaded his eyes and peered at the landing party. He dropped his shovel and ran forward. " Bress de Lord, dere is the great messiah! I knowed him as soon as I seed him. He's bin in my heart fo' long years an' he's cum at las' to free his children from bondage! Glory, Hallelujah! " He kneeled to kiss the President's feet, and the other Negroes followed his lead.

" Don't kneel to me," Lincoln said to them. " That is not right. You must kneel to God only, and thank Him for the liberty you will hereafter enjoy. I am but God's humble instrument; but you may rest assured that as long as I live no one shall put a shackle on your limbs, and you shall have all the rights which God has given to every other free citizen of this Republic."

[1] As is true of so many events associated with Lincoln's visit to Richmond, the time of arrival is not definite. The New York *Herald* reported him at Rockett's " early in the day." The *Herald* of April 5 stated that Admiral Farragut and his party reached Richmond at 8:30 A.M. The Admiral visited Weitzel and other officers, toured the city, and sailed from Rockett's on the *William Allison*. Shortly after weighing anchor he met the presidential barge ascending the river. On the basis of this evidence, Lincoln could have landed at eleven, if Farragut stayed in the city only two and a half hours. Emma Mordecai, who wrote her recollections on the fifth, has the President arriving in the afternoon. J. B. Jones gives the hour as 4:00 P. M., but he confused the time of arrival with the time of the President's tour of Richmond. Putnam has him walking up Main Street at 11:00 A. M., Porter does not mention the hour, and Sandburg has the President in Richmond in time to lunch with Weitzel at the Confederate White House.

Porter urged, then ordered the Negroes to leave. He entreated them to let the President proceed. " Yes, Massa," the old man said, " but after bein' so many years in the desert without water, its mighty pleasant to be lookin' at las' on our spring of life. 'Scuse us, sir; we means no disrespec' to Massa Lincoln; we means all love and gratitude." The Negroes joined hands and sang a melodious old hymn. Drawn by the music, other Negroes came running from hovels and side streets. Some came tumbling and shouting; others remained silent and awed. They thronged around Lincoln, to get a look at him, to shake his hand, or to hear the tone of his voice.

On Porter's order twelve men of the boat's crew fixed bayonets and surrounded the President. Lincoln held his little son by the hand and started up Main Street. He walked with a long awkward stride. He carried one shoulder higher than the other, and both seemed too sloping for his height. One strong arm swung by his side, and his skin was tanned from days in the sun at City Point. His forehead was wide and high, his gray-brown eyes were sunken under thick eyebrows, his nose was straight and prominent, and little furrows extended from his mouth across his cheeks. Mrs. Pryor recalled him as tired, old, and the " ugliest man I ever saw." But to the Negroes and to some white people, who paraded and shouted around him, Lincoln represented the beauty of freedom and the emblem of peace. From time to time he removed his hat and fanned his face. In the warm sun perspiration trickled down his brow and cheeks.

Slowly the small procession pushed through the crowd. Half an hour passed before Libby Prison came in view. Lincoln stopped to look at the former prison of Union officers.

" We'll pull it down," the people cried.

" No," the President said, " leave it as a monument."

Porter searched the street for a Federal soldier, but he saw none. He considered it useless to send a message to Weitzel by one of the celebrating Negroes. A white man in shirt sleeves rushed from the sidewalk toward Lincoln. The guards tensed; but the man stopped and said: " Abraham Lincoln, God bless you: You are the poor man's friend." He pushed forward, but being restrained by guards, he threw his hat into the air in exultation. A pretty seventeen-year-old girl came forward with a bouquet in her hands. The jostling crowd pulled her dress askew. Attached to her flowers was a card: " From Eva to the liberator of the slaves." A Negro mother lifted her child above the massed heads so that he could see the " savior." An old man turned away in disgust, mumbling that this ordinary-looking farmer could not be the President of the United States.

At last Porter saw a Federal cavalryman sitting on his horse, and asked him to get the President an escort from General Weitzel. The soldier stared for a moment. " Is that Old Abe? " he asked before turning his mount toward head-quarters.

At Fourteenth Street the party turned north to avoid the debris on Main, and moved west along Franklin to Governor Street. A detachment of cavalry arrived at last with a clatter of hoofs; it wheeled about and led the procession. Now the crowd followed the President. Window shutters flew open in this better residential area so that the curious could see. From some distance Lincoln made a commanding appearance in his high silk hat and long black coat. A bodyguard thought he saw the glint of a gun in a second story window and stepped in front of the President. A spectator turned from a window and told someone, " The Old Ape is here." The presidential party moved rapidly up Twelfth Street and turned right onto Marshall and went on to the entry of the

From Leslie's Illustrated History of the Civil War

PRESIDENT LINCOLN
Riding Through Richmond on the Afternoon of April 4

former residence of Jefferson Davis.[2] The crowd cheered Lincoln, and after he entered the house, the people added a few more for Admiral Porter.

Lincoln seemed " pale, haggard, and utterly worn out " as he sank into a chair and asked for a glass of water. Refreshed, he inspected the house, teetered in Davis' chair, and fingered small mantle decorations. He received and conferred with Weitzel and the officers of his staff. A servant brought in a bottle of old whiskey, and it was passed around to willing hands. Everyone but Lincoln took swigs until the bottle was empty. The President rested while servants prepared lunch.

After a simple meal he started a busy afternoon with an informal reception for Union officers. Lincoln wished to talk with some prominent Southerners. Judge Campbell pleaded for the South and told the President: ". . . when leniency and cruelty play for conquest of a kingdom the gentlest player will be the soonest winner." He said that many prominent Virginians, if called together by Lincoln, would restore Virginia to the Union. This possibility interested Lincoln, and he asked Campbell to visit him the next morning on the *Malvern.* Campbell kept the appointment and thought the President " exhibited a broad, liberal, generous and mag-

[2] In his unreliable reminiscences Admiral Porter stated that Lincoln walked from Rockett's to the Confederate White House. Putnam declares that a superb carriage was in readiness for him at Capitol Square. An entry in Jones's *Diary* has Lincoln in a carriage drawn by four horses, but Jones was evidently describing the President's afternoon tour of Richmond. In her *Reminiscences of Peace and War* (New York, London, 1904) Mrs. Pryor follows Jones. Sandburg has the President walking, and Clifford Dowdey gives him a ride. Certainly he walked from Rockett's to Capitol Square. Possibly he rode from the square to the Confederate White House, but it is doubtful that General Weitzel or his subordinates secured a carriage and four on such short notice and in the confusion of the occupation. A carriage was used for the afternoon trip of the President.

nanimous form of settlement " for Southerners. Lincoln demanded the restoration of the Union, abolition of slavery, and the disbanding of all hostile forces as acts necessary for peace. Rather than confiscating additional property of Southerners, the President would restore their property to all who promptly laid down their arms. According to Campbell, Lincoln suggested calling the Virginia legislature into session to break the state's tie with the Confederacy. Later the President authorized General Weitzel to call the Virginia legislators, but the surrender of General Lee at Appomattox made this action unnecessary.[3]

After completing his afternoon conferences on April 4, Lincoln rode around the city in an open carriage. With an escort of Negro cavalry he saw the historic and the burnt in Richmond. On Capitol Square advance riders cleared a path through a cheering crowd as the " carriage and four " moved slowly around the walks. Everywhere his reception was the

[3] Campbell claimed he did not suggest calling the Virginia legislature. He urged the President to call a number of Virginia leaders, but Lincoln hoped the legislature would repeal the ordinance of seccession and take Virginia out of the war. With their state out of the conflict, the President thought Lee and other Virginians would surrender. Campbell described his meetings with Lincoln in a letter to Horace Greeley on April 26, and in his amnesty petition of June 22, 1865 (Campbell-Colson Papers, Southern Collection, University of North Carolina) Campbell stated that the account of the meetings as published in the New York *Tribune* on April 22, 1865, was inaccurate.

Carl Sandburg (*Abraham Lincoln: The War Years*, IV, 179-80) has stated that Lincoln asked to see Roger A. Pryor, but the latter refused to confer with the President on the grounds that he was a paroled officer of a country still at war with the United States. In reality Pryor was not in Richmond. The day before, in Petersburg, Lincoln had sent for Pryor, " But General Pryor excused himself, saying that he was a paroled prisoner of war, that General Lee was still in the field, and that he could hold no conference with the head of the opposing army." (Mrs. Roger Pryor, *Reminiscences of Peace and War*, 353.)

same—hands reaching to him, voices raised in praise, accompanied by the martial music of bands. Along the various routes Negroes saluted their idol, and many Southern white people joined them in tribute. According to the wife of General George Pickett, she answered a knock on her door that afternoon, and holding her squirming child, she said that her husband was not at home. " I know where he is," the tall man replied. Lincoln introduced himself and told Mrs. Pickett of a former day when he had known young Pickett and of his law partner who had obtained an appointment to West Point for the now-famous Confederate general. The President kissed the baby and said goodbye.

Lincoln did not spend the night in the Confederate White House. Porter's flagship, the *Malvern*, had navigated the river and was anchored in the James. Admiral Porter urged the President to sleep on shipboard that night, and he breathed more freely when Lincoln was safe and protected on the ship. The visit to occupied but hostile Richmond was a foolhardy act; but the President wanted it. Ten days hence his life would be in its ultimate jeopardy at Ford's Theater in Washington.

A New Order

FROM THE DECK of the *Malvern* Lincoln saw a peaceful city. Already new economic life stirred in Richmond. The pontoon bridge across the James was nearing completion, and the progress made in repairing railways gave promise of early mail service and revived trade. The transition from depreciated currency and inflated prices to Federal bills and reasonable rates was already accomplished. Sutler's stores were pleasant oases of supply in sections of the war-weary city. Residents without money bartered their silver services and gold ornaments for groceries and clothing. Soldiers bought commemorative medals, such as a bar pin stamped " U. S. Grant " with " Capture of Richmond, April 3, 1865 " on a dangling disk.

The Richmond *Whig* appeared as a Union paper, and on the night of April 4 Richmond people read accounts of the previous day's fire in its columns. In reality occupation was less of a trial than most people had expected. The feared pillage by Yankees never materialized. Even without the institution of slavery the Negroes remained well behaved. People were hungry, but there was promise of more in peace than in war. Old, familiar procedures gradually returned. An Episcopalian picked up a prewar prayer book for family prayers and read the petition for the President of the United States. " Oh Papa," his daughter exclaimed. " You prayed for the President of the United States." " Did I! " her father replied. " Devil fetch him." And the family laughed.

Judge Campbell philosophized at his desk. He saw that the overthrow of the political doctrines and social system of the Southern states was a mighty revolution in the South. The success of the North created a new order. Northern principles, opinions, social, political, and economic systems now predominated and in the future would increase in strength. Wise and moderate statesmen, Campbell hoped, would be content with their triumph.

An unseen bugler lifted his trumpet above Richmond. Taps sounded below the Potomac for an indefensible system of human bondage and a unique way of life but announced a future industrial economy of relative plenty. The occupied city grieved for the old while moving painfully toward distant and greater glory in a reunited America.

A NOTE ON SOURCES

Published diaries, reminiscences, biographies, mono-
graphs, and general accounts of the Confederacy, Richmond,
and individuals associated with the Federal and Confederate
governments are listed in standard works and bibliographies.
All of these sources were consulted, but few writers give
more than sentences or paragraphs to the fall of Richmond.
After the Civil War the evacuation and occupation of the
city were popular topics for decades in the literary magazines of the United States. Many of these articles are reminiscences and must be used with care, for they give conflict-
ing accounts of the three days in April of 1865. In recalling
their roles during those days authors were more interested in
defending or exalting themselves than in giving accurate
accounts of events. Recollections of participants in and observers of dramatic actions are usually faulty in spite of the
attempted honesty of the writer.

Those first days of April in Richmond bustled with
activity. There was little time for contemplation or the
recording of scenes, and the disruption of mail service discouraged residents from writing about the events in Richmond for the benefit of absent friends or relatives. Therefore, few letters are available and even the voluminous *War
of The Rebellion . . . Official Records of the Union and
Confederate Armies* contain little more than bare facts.
However, some letters, diaries, and reminiscences were written during or within a few days after the occupation of Rich-

mond. The best of these in the Southern Historical Collection at the University of North Carolina are: Emma Mordecai's " Diary, May, 1864—May, 1865 "; the John A. Campbell-George R. Colston Papers; Anna Holmes Trenholm's " Diary "; Anita Dwyer Withers' " Diary, May 1860—June, 1865 "; James W. Albright's " Diary," Volume II, January–April, 1865; Edward Hitchcock McDonald's "Reminiscences" written in January, 1866; and the Isaac C. Richardson Letters, 1862–1865. Although written years after the fall of Richmond, Berry Greenwood Benson's " Reminiscences," James R. Sheldon's " The Last March of the Army of Lee," Peter Helms Mayo's " Recollections," George Alexander Martin's " Memoir of the Demise of the Confederacy," and Leeland Hathaway's " Recollections," all of which are in the Southern Historical Collection, are important sources. The Elizabeth Van Lew Papers in the Manuscript Division of the New York Public Library contain fragments of notes which she kept as well as a part of her reminiscences.

Newspaper reporters entered Richmond with the Federal army of occupation. From April 3 until the assassination of President Lincoln the leading Northern metropolitan newspapers carried detailed accounts of the people and the conditions in Richmond. The Boston, New York, Philadelphia, Baltimore, Washington, Cincinnati, and Chicago newspapers are the most valuable sources of information for this study. After it resumed publication on April 4, 1865, the Richmond *Whig* gave column after column to the fall of the city. In later weeks and years other newspapers of Richmond printed eyewitness accounts and reminiscences of Northern and Southern participants in the evacuation and occupation of the Confederate capital.

INDEX

THE WALTER LYNWOOD FLEMING
LECTURES IN SOUTHERN HISTORY